Praise for *The Reset Button*

"*The Reset Button* is a game-changer for anyone ready to rewrite their story. Cameo shares raw, relatable, real-life experiences with vulnerability and courage, inspiring you to move away from your comfort zone, face your own fears and flaws, embrace change, and take ownership and bold action in your life. If you're ready to take your life to the next level, this book is a must-read."

JESSE ITZLER, Entrepreneur, *New York Times* bestselling author, endurance athlete, and part-owner of the Atlanta Hawks

"Brave, bold, and filled with the perfect blend of relatable real talk and inspiration, this book will give you the courage to confront your deepest fears and build a life that reflects who you really are—even if you've made mistakes, been knocked around in life, and truly despise change."

JUDI HOLLER, Keynote speaker and bestselling author of *Fear Is My Homeboy*

"Raw, powerful, and profoundly inspiring exploration of personal transformation. With candid honesty and heartfelt reflection, Cameo takes us on a journey from a seemingly perfect façade to a life of genuine fulfillment and authenticity. Her experiences are a testament to the power of self-discovery and the possibility of real change. This book is a must-read for anyone ready to take charge of their own path to fulfillment and happiness."

DESIREE WODICKER, Pro Muay Thai fighter, mentor, speaker, and founder of Pantera Wealth

"Cameo goes there! With vulnerability and honesty, she reflects on the parenting mistakes she made and the actionable strategies she uses to fix those mistakes and connect at a deeper level with her kids. A must-read for any parent who feels their kids need to act a specific way to be successful—and your kids are fighting you every step of the way—Cameo's honesty will comfort you and lead you to create change in your own life."

JOANN CROHN, M.ED., founder, parent coach, and podcast host of *No Guilt Mom*

the reset button

REFLECT, RESET,
AND REINVENT YOUR LIFE

CAMEO ELYSE BRAUN

The Reset Button is a work of nonfiction. The people, places, events, and experiences are presented to the best of the author's recollection. Nonetheless, some names and identifying details have been changed. Any similarities to real persons, living or deceased, are purely coincidental.

Copyright ©2025 by Cameo Elyse Braun
Published by Snowy Egret Press
Bradenton, Florida

All rights reserved. No part of this book may be copied, stored, or shared in any form—whether electronic, mechanical, photographic, or otherwise—without written permission from the publisher or author, except for brief excerpts used in reviews or articles.

This book is not intended as medical or psychological advice. It is not a substitute for professional care or treatment. The author's intent is to share general information and personal experiences to support readers on their journey to well-being. Always consult a qualified professional for health-related concerns.

Hardcover ISBN: 979-8-9918572-1-5
Paperback ISBN: 979-8-9918572-0-8
eBook ISBN: 979-8-9918572-2-2

Cataloging-in-Publication Date is on file at the Library of Congress

Cover and interior design by Vanessa Mendozzi

Bulk purchases for schools, businesses, and organizations may be available at special rates. For inquiries, contact, email hello@cameoelysebraun.com.

Printed in the United States of America.

For Faith and Ben

Always know that you are the best part of my life and the light that has kept me going on the hardest days. May you always have the curiosity & courage to become who you're meant to be, the grace to forgive yourselves along the way, and the agility to pivot when needed.

CONTENTS

Introduction. **When the Shit Hits the Proverbial Fan**   1

SECTION 1. RESETTING YOURSELF

Introduction. **Resetting Yourself. Initial Thoughts**   11

1. Resetting Yourself. **Begin at the Beginning...**   15

2. Resetting Yourself. **Blinking Into Marriage and Motherhood**   29

3. Resetting Yourself. **Losing My Identity**   43

4. Resetting Yourself. **Hitting the Reset Button on Ourselves**   61

→ *Hit the Reset Button on Yourself*   *76*

SECTION 2. RESETTING YOUR MARRIAGE OR PARTNERSHIP

Introduction. **Resetting Your Marriage or Partnership. Initial Thoughts**   85

5. Resetting Your Marriage or Partnership. **The Rockiest Bottom**   89

6. Resetting Your Marriage or Partnership. **Miscommunication**   101

7. Resetting Your Marriage or Partnership. **The Intimacy Personality Test**   111

8. Resetting Your Marriage or Partnership. **Hitting the Reset Button on Your Relationship**   121

→ *Hit the Reset Button on Your Relationship*   *130*

SECTION 3. RESETTING HOW YOU DEAL WITH YOUR SHIT... TOXIC COPING STRATEGIES

Introduction. **Resetting How You Deal with Your Shit. Initial Thoughts**   137

9. Resetting How You Deal with Your Shit. **Coping Habits**   141

10. Resetting How You Deal with Your Shit. **Doing It One Day at a Time**   151

11. Resetting How You Deal with Your Shit. **Hitting the Reset Button on Toxic Coping Strategies**   163

→ *Hit the Reset Button on How You Deal with Your Shit*   *173*

SECTION 4. THE RESET RIPPLE EFFECT ON PARENTING AND CAREER

Introduction. **The Reset Ripple Effect on Parenting and Career or All You Others. Initial Thoughts**   183

12. Hitting the Reset Button on Parenting. **Because I Said So**   185

→ *Hit the Reset Button on Parenting*   *193*

13. Hitting the Reset Button on Your Career. **Working It Out**   203

→ *Hit the Reset Button on Your Career*   *214*

SECTION 5. MAINTENANCE

Introduction. **Maintenance. Initial Thoughts**   223

14. Maintenance. **Leaning on that Reset Button**   225

15. Maintenance. **You Got This**   233

Acknowledgements   237

About the Author   243

INTRODUCTION

WHEN THE SHIT HITS THE PROVERBIAL FAN

The perfect life.
The perfect marriage.
The perfect mom.
The perfect BMW.
The perfect boob job.

Appearances are something, aren't they? When anyone would jokingly mention, "Cameo, you've got it all," I would smile and nod and agree. Of course I would agree. It would be rude not to. After all, I was working so hard at selling all that perfection to the outside world, how could I not enthusiastically indulge their assumption? I was a mom with two healthy kids—ages three and eight—the wife of a charming family man, the keeper of an always tidy home, a runner, and a budding competitive bodybuilder. I was Cameo, the queen of the playdate and the life of the grown-up party. My husband, Greg, was my best bud and we shared a large circle of friends in our perfect Ohio suburb. I had, ostensibly, arrived.

It was all "perfect-y" and true.

But here's what else was true: I was angry. Bitter. Driven by my ego. Underneath that fit body and the perky boobs, I was struggling. Sad. Rotting. My sense of self was wilting rapidly as the demand for me to switch hats, switch roles, switch the

The Reset Button

definition of who I needed to be increased. Woman. Wife. Stay-at-home-mother, and then working mother. Competitive bodybuilder. Kid playmate. Leader of the drunken revelers. On and on. As the list grew, my sense of self shrank. But I told myself I had everything a girl could want. What did it matter if it took a glass of wine (or a bottle) at the end of each day to convince myself that I was genuinely happy?

Like many other women, depending on whether my kids' needs or our financial needs took precedence, I had to bounce between being a full-time working mom and a full-time stay-at-home mom. In both roles I felt like I was doing too much and not enough. I also demanded of myself that I be the best at whatever I did, but then I resented it when nobody noticed my efforts. Neither job felt fulfilling and both relegated me to the background. For a person used to being the star—competitive athlete, straight A student, social MVP—I was ill-suited to life as a bit player. Yet, I didn't know how to communicate my overwhelming sadness and dissatisfaction. More than that, I thought I wasn't allowed to ask for anything for myself, and when I did, I could feel Greg's resentment at upending our carefully mapped out family schedule. So my identity—the one not tied to any labels like mom or wife, the one that was just about me—began to disappear.

Some people, when faced with intense unhappiness, might wither and go through the motions of their life. Some might break down. Not me. I partied. I drank. And then when that wasn't enough, I rebelled.

I started having an affair.

My affair wasn't about being in love. It wasn't about running away together to begin a new life. Those things were never even options. I was just won over by the lightness of it all. I savored my escapes less because of who I was escaping with and more because it provided me a respite from all the pressures of being Cameo the Mom and Cameo the Wife. I convinced myself that the affair was so innocent, so meaningless, that it didn't matter. This allowed me to compartmentalize my betrayal.

I continued my efforts at trying to be the perfect mom, the best wife, and the amazing Cameo, while also sneaking away for short adventures where I got to be the center of attention. And while my little escapades brought some relief from my sadness, I still felt frustrated and unappreciated—and now also guilty. But I stayed quiet in my animosity. I muted all the yuck and let it simmer underneath my *I-can-handle-it-all-and-refuse-to-admit-any-weakness* smile. Greg could often sense my silent anger. And, when he couldn't, I would explode and throw an irrational fit. Unsurprisingly, this only succeeded in making things worse and earned me the title of Bat-Shit-Crazy. After these episodes I would close myself off, feeling hurt, dismissed, and misunderstood. But instead of confronting those feelings, I would misdirect them through self-destructive behaviors or onto another distraction. My resentment toward Greg was building, which pulled me further away from him. I began drinking more heavily and more frequently, and I threw my attention into whatever was put in front of me at whatever moment. It all only compounded my problems and became an awful cycle.

As bad went to worse and private marital turbulence became public (especially when booze was involved), a friend suggested couples counseling. Both individually driven by our indomitable desires for validation, we reluctantly decided to give it a try.

Over time, to our surprise, our sessions with the therapist began paying off. Greg and I were working hard at communicating more thoughtfully with each other. Things started coming up that we'd both been brushing under the rug for years. Some of it was typical—tension about family involvement and disagreements about household responsibilities—and some of it was more unique to us—our heavy reliance on weekend binge drinking and partying. Having an unbiased moderator ensured that we listened openly and without defensiveness—even when something felt unfair.

I know what you must be wondering: When in our sessions did my ongoing affair come up? When did I admit my active duplicity? Here's the truth: I never did. The affair just seemed completely separate from my real life. I told myself that revealing it would only hurt Greg and distract us from our real problems. However misguided, that is truly what I believed. It was difficult enough for me to soften my "I don't need any help" tough-girl façade; there was no way I could also admit to this huge failure of judgment. And more than anything, I wanted Greg and me to live happily ever after. So I kept that part of my life secret.

On the surface it was all working out so well, until Greg sat me down one fall morning and told me we needed to talk. He'd been distant for a couple of days and had stayed home from work, so I knew something was brewing. Our daughter was at school and our son was napping upstairs when he gestured for me to sit down at the kitchen table. He sat in the chair across from me, unable to make eye contact. His gaze was fixed on some notes he was tightly gripping. Notes? I noticed also that his hands were shaking. Believe it or not, I had no idea what he was about to say. I waited. Finally, he came out with it: "I know you're having an affair."

My heart sank into my stomach and everything I had so neatly compartmentalized in my mind suddenly converged into one intricate mess.

It was at this moment that I fully comprehended how my deception, my self-indulgence, and my anger had brought my marriage, my family, and my sense of self to their knees. I knew there would be no going back, so I had to figure out in what way I would be moving forward.

Eventually I realized that what I really needed was a transformation.

I needed to stop playing at being perfect and sink in to being human. I needed to feel the weight of my mistakes and own them, learn from them. What I wanted was the chance to rebuild and renovate how I lived my life and interacted with the world around me. Essentially, what I needed was a metaphorical reset button. But that's impossible, right? You can't just reset your life, can you?

Here's what I discovered. You absolutely can. And in this book, I'm going to tell you how.

The Reset Button. It's a concept that began as a whisper and has grown louder with every decision that brought me closer to living a life of purpose and fulfillment. The Reset Button has allowed me to take complete ownership of my life. It helped Greg and me transform a failing marriage into a thriving, loving partnership. It has shaken me out of a dead-end career and given me the courage to start my own businesses. It has introduced me to more opportunities and happiness than I've ever experienced within myself and in my relationships. And, maybe most importantly, it has allowed me to take charge of where I'm heading, without worrying about whether it's what I think I "should" be doing. The Reset Button is also a way to acknowledge and then move on from past mistakes.

Just to be clear, this concept isn't about a one-time Hard Reset. It isn't a tool to be used recklessly or reactively in difficult situations. It isn't a redo. It's about reflecting on how you're currently living versus how you *want* to be living and then developing a plan and practice to move you one step closer to the latter. It's about being brave enough to say "this isn't working for me" and determining what will. It's a reorientation for your thought process that can change the outcome of your decisions for the better. And not every change needs to be big. Resetting even small everyday choices can add up to huge overall changes.

Who needs a reset? Who doesn't? The Reset Button is for anyone who's ready to shake up how they're living. Maybe you are desperate for a change but don't quite have a good starting strategy. Maybe change has been thrust upon you and you feel like a reinvention is in order. Maybe you've just been feeling this nebulous Life Malaise or pain from past trauma that you can't address with brutal honesty. Or maybe, like I did, you need to find your identity again. Whatever the reason, the Reset Button will get you thinking more intelligently about not just your choices but also *the why* behind them.

Over the years I've applied some part of this practice of a Reset Button to just about every area of my life. I've primarily used it on myself and my marriage and then allowed those changes to trickle down into the other parts of my life. Doing this work has naturally altered the way I handled my career and parented my children. This practice has been so effective and resulted in such a positive and apparent shift in my life and my relationships that a number of friends and family members have asked how they can make similar changes in their own lives. That's where the idea of writing this book came in. In *The Reset Button*, I walk through how I reset every part of my life. First, how I reset myself—how I made decisions, organized my priorities, and worked on managing my ego. I reset my marriage—working with Greg to balance one another's needs, how to show love, and how to communicate more honestly. And, to put it bluntly, I reset how I dealt with my shit—letting go of the toxic coping strategies I held on to. I also offer advice on ways to reset your career and parenting choices. The best part is whatever area(s) of your life you apply this practice to, I think you'll find that it'll organically reshape other areas as well.

There are three parts within the Reset Button: the Reflection, the Reset, and the Reinvention. Do one without the others, and it all falls flat. Commit to all three and you'll discover true and lasting change. With each section, I want to share with you how this practice, and the three steps within it, can wholly alter things for the better.

Let's look at these 3Rs.

The Reflection: We've all been there: those moments where we furiously rationalize something that we know just doesn't feel right. It's that twinge in your belly. The goose bumps on your arms. The mental alarm bells. Or maybe it's that little voice who warned you not to sing that Beyoncé song at karaoke with your coworkers. Wherever it's coming from, I'm sure you can recall a consequence of not listening to that feeling. A time when you thought to yourself, *I knew this was a bad idea*. Once you get into the habit of reflecting on that instinct, you'll bring more awareness to it and start taking it seriously. The Reflection can often feel uncomfortable. It forces you to swim against the current, but it's also a moment that forces you to grow.

The Reset: Permission, baby. This is the moment where you open yourself up to that new possibility. Your willingness to press Reset greases the wheels of change. We all get so used to how we've been doing things and why we've been doing things a certain way that we never stop to think, hey, maybe I don't actually have to continue doing this thing or acting this way or making this choice. The Reset is the ability to be open to new approaches and/or new perspectives. It removes limits and excites that sense of curiosity that often goes dormant as we get older.

The Reinvention: This is the good stuff. It's the courage to break through the barriers of who you think you should be and *finally* get to who you really are. Choosing things based on what will make you happier, what you need, what will help your family, and what will help you feel more fulfilled. The Reinvention is the *doing* part.

The Reset Button can provide the secret sauce to a life that's lived *your* way. I'm not here to weigh in on the decisions you're making; I'm here to share a helpful formula on how to make them. I was only able to figure it out after hitting my personal rock bottom, but if I can prevent someone else from hitting theirs, then sharing my story will all be worth it. My hope is that, as you practice hitting your own Reset Button, it will inspire you to take an ongoing inventory of your life. Commit to the practice and it'll effect change that will open the doors to living up to your truest potential.

Bonus: It also makes life a lot more fun!

SECTION 1

Resetting Yourself

INTRODUCTION

RESETTING YOURSELF

Initial Thoughts

Before we dive eyeballs-first into the *You* in Resetting Yourself, I want to make a few quick points. As many of you already probably know, you can't truly make any meaningful changes in other areas of your life without first having an understanding of yourself. When I hit the Reset Button for myself, I had to go way back to my past to figure out how I'd habituated and learned certain behaviors and practices. And when I say "figure out," I mean a full comprehension and investigation of those layers beneath our most shallow level. All too often we accept the version of self that has been formed by unhealed traumas from our past or from stories cultivated and embedded in our mind by others. When my marriage was on the line, I had to first step back and take a long hard stink-eye-stare at myself before I could address what was going on in my relationship. I realized that in order to make positive changes in my partnership with Greg I had to 1) be open to the idea that I was the cause of some of our issues (which my ego was not happy about) and 2) figure out where those issues were stemming from. I like to think of the popular metaphor (that I believe was first coined by AA) of *keeping my side of the street clean*. It's a great way to remind myself about my own responsibility in everything. The more honest we are with ourselves, the more we can fully realize what triggers the reactions/decisions/outbursts that lead us astray. And the best thing about understanding your triggers is that you can quell the usual ugly aftermath of said provocation. No havoc wreaking, no tornado of emotion, and no saying things you know you'll regret. And that equals a nice clean street.

The second point I want to make has to do with how we talk to ourselves in comparison to how we talk to others. Ever notice how much more critical we are with ourselves than we are with friends? We can be so unabashedly brutal to ourselves in ways that we would never dare to be with others. That mental critic who points out all the things on our to-do list that we didn't get to or all the mistakes we made during the day goes on mute when a friend has similar missteps or transgressions. It can be scary in our own head, can't it? It's funny how we all root for the underdog and celebrate a comeback story, yet we'll go to bed feeling like an utter failure because we forgot our kid had Pajama Day and we sent them to school in normal clothes. I point this out because, as you read this section, you may find yourself feeling empathy and compassion for me and my situation. Learning about the context of my story and reading about some of the experiences I had as a kid might bring clarity and depth to the choices I made. Knowing my backstory will likely breed understanding and kindness from you, even though you might never forgive yourself had you made the same decisions and mistakes that I did. You know your own backstory better than anyone. I'm hoping that this book will be your first step in quieting that critic in your head and learning to offer compassion and kindness to yourself. Maybe you can even open yourself up to the idea that you are your very own comeback story.

Another point I want to make has to do with overlap. The different parts of our lives are not lived in a vacuum. Analyzing the same events from different vantage points can help you parse out the root causes behind the choices you're making. But that inevitably leads to some overlap. Our relationship with ourselves bleeds into our partnerships, which bleeds into how we parent and on and on. I've done my best to try to focus each section on that one specific area in my life, but I'm sure you'll notice how treating myself differently has naturally led to different parenting choices and a shift in how I interact with others. My affair appears in just about every section, but how it applies to my personal growth as opposed to my marriage (or my career or my parenting) is different. So just as the different parts of our lives are not lived in a vacuum, neither are the choices we make. The great thing about this is that, while there were specific changes I needed to make in every single area of my life, I found that adjusting one part organically brought benefits to others. I like to think of this as the Reset Ripple Effect.

Lastly, I fully understand that digging deep and figuring out "the why" for ourselves takes work. While I initially chose therapy (among other things), that doesn't have to be the answer for everyone. I talk more about healthy outlets in the Deal with Your Shit section, but I encourage you to begin thinking about ways in which you can safely investigate "the why" for yourself. If it's not therapy, then maybe it's meditation or going for a run or journaling. Treat yourself to a safe space of your own choosing and start your very own personal reset.

Enjoy the ride.

RESETTING YOURSELF

Begin at the Beginning...

When my marriage to Greg imploded I was forced to do something I had avoided for much of my life—examine my childhood. I was never a particularly introspective adult—or kid for that matter. My way of handling things was by pushing through, partying, and fixating on whatever goal I was working toward at the time. But I've since realized that the better I understand the Why and Where of my habits and behaviors, the easier time I have at making changes. Wearing my Bat-Shit-Crazy-Lady cape no longer makes sense when I understand what has set me off in the first place. More importantly, understanding the Why has helped me be a better advocate for myself. It's powerful when you acknowledge that your behavior, even if it's unproductive, is rooted in an event(s) that was imprinted on your brain years ago. After putting a ton of work in, I realized that, up until my almost-divorce, I was handling conflicts and unhappiness the exact same way I handled them when I was a kid. Maturity be damned.

I should say that my childhood, generally speaking, was a great one. I was one of those lucky kids who always understood that I was loved and had people in my corner. Up until the age of about

The Reset Button

thirteen, we lived in a tiny, rural town in Ohio where there was one two-way intersection and that was it. It was the type of place where the kids spent their days running around outside barefoot and dirty. Where church was the social center and a grocery store was twenty minutes away. It seemed like everyone knew everyone else and, more than that, that we were all related somehow. My grandparents on my mom's side, my mom's aunt and uncle, as well as her brother's family and his kids were all close by. I was an only child but had plenty of playmates available to me. House hopping was a regular form of entertainment.

We lived in a double-wide trailer. It's funny, but I didn't realize that fact until I was older. Maybe I always assumed it was a house because it wasn't in a trailer park community. Or maybe because my dad put a foundation on a portion of it. Then again, maybe it was simply my home, so the fact that it was a trailer didn't matter. My parents were always doing what they could to make it as nice as possible. From renovations to landscaping to the countless hours my mom put into cleaning, they spent a lot of downtime making the best of it. For as far back as I can remember, my mom's Friday nights were spent scrubbing every inch of our home—including the baseboards. Ever wonder if there are *really* people out there who wash their walls? Not me. I know for sure there are. I'm related to one of them. To this day, every time I look at the dusty baseboards in my own grown-ass adult-lady house, I'm reminded of the right-way/wrong-way philosophy both of my parents continue to live by.

I loved being an only child. The lone-wolf lifestyle suited me: no sharing, the regular spotlight, and alone time whenever I craved it. It forced me to develop a sense of creativity and independence. I used to set up our camera and film myself performing sing-alongs. Sometimes I'd disappear on adventures until my parents would yell for me to come home. Other times, they'd find me sitting on the porch of our elderly neighbor, Wilbur, chatting away and drinking coffee-milk with him. Being a party of one also afforded me special treatment within our extended family. My grandpa would take me along to scope out garage sales, but not before we stopped for breakfast at the local diner to eat and shoot-the-shit with his buddies. I loved it. My cousins, who all had siblings, never got that special time with him.

My parents did their very best to celebrate and encourage my endeavors. From performing onstage, to piano and singing lessons, to playing sports, to every other activity in between, my mom and dad enabled me to participate in all of it. From the age of five until about fifteen, they carted me to and from piano lessons and then, when I was good enough, they brought me to competitions where I would play long classical pieces for judges who were grading me on things like finger placement, sitting position, dynamics, and tempo. That commitment was matched by my dedication to sports and athletics, which often required practices before and after school. Looking back, I marvel at how much scheduling and planning they had to do to support all of my interests. When they couldn't cart me back and forth themselves, they got relatives, friends, and even teachers to help out. I was the star of their lives and I relished it.

By around age nine, however, things started to shift, and I became aware of a lot of tension and resentment among our extended family. This was around the time that both my mom and dad suffered the loss of a parent. On my mom's side, it was her mother. On my dad's, it was the stepfather who had been like a father to him.

Death brings grief, but it also often brings out animosity. Any protective layer that had previously been covering our extended family's long-held hurts was ripped away by the sadness of loss. I can recall nasty messages on our answering machine and angry letters from relatives on both sides. Since I was a kid at the time, I don't remember the details of the arguments, but I do remember the tension. It seemed like everything changed from then on. Lines were drawn, then redrawn, and redrawn again. I couldn't keep up with who was being iced out and who had made it back into the fold. I learned quickly that familial relationships were not unconditional. People could love you one minute and hate you the next. This put a semipermanent crack in my idea of what a family was.

It always seemed as if my parents' way of dealing with all the drama was simply to ignore it as much as humanly possible. They pushed through. They worked. They tried not to ruffle feathers. It was all pressed down and hidden away. Any torment the fighting caused always seemed to get buried beneath the happenings of the day, the to-do list, and the cleaning and fixing of the house.

Until I was a teenager, it felt like my mom and dad were best friends. They were a team. Up until the age of thirteen, when we lived in that trailer, I can't remember them ever really fighting—aside from minuscule bickering and short-lived arguments. Now that I'm older however, I realize they were probably disregarding many things that deserved their attention. The space between them must have been crowded with all of the metaphorical elephants in the room.

One point of tension that was never talked about with any depth was the fact that my grandmother on my dad's side couldn't stand my mom. Minus the sporadic (and confusing) moments when she played nice, my grandmother essentially refused to acknowledge my mom's existence. She even went so far as to invite my dad and me over for family gatherings but not extend the invitation to my mom. It seems outrageous when I think about it now, but I don't recall there ever being a debate about whether to refuse my grandmother or push back at all. My mom never even seemed very upset or hurt. In fact, I think she may have even reluctantly encouraged him to go in an attempt to do the "right thing." I know it's possible that my parents could have discussed the issue in private, but I truly don't think they ever did. I believe they handled it the same way they handled most other things—by pretending all of it was fine. For my dad in particular, his end goal was simply to keep everyone happy. Don't make waves. Don't create chaos. These were the mottos that he lived by. So he and I would occasionally celebrate with his family without my mom there. Or he would just not attend the gathering at all. No fuss was ever made about why he wasn't going. And that kept the peace, at least on one side.

In my grandmother's eyes, the stigma that my mom carried would sometimes extend to me as well. Whereas she would attend my cousins' games and performances, she never paid attention to any of my activities. She gave gifts to them but not to me. But again, it was never talked about or addressed. It just was what it was, so I went along thinking it was normal.

Telling myself "it is what it is" was how I learned to handle things. For example, once the grandmother on my mom's side passed, my grandfather—the one who let me pal around with his friends and journey with him from garage sale to garage sale—left. He moved away. From then on, I never saw him with any regularity. But like my parents, I dealt with it by simply ignoring the impact that this had on me. I never addressed it with anyone or processed how I felt about him leaving. I also never thought to tell my dad's mother that it hurt not to have my mom be with us for family get-togethers or that it made me sad that she gave my cousins gifts but not me.

I just kept moving forward.

My process was not to process anything. By the time I was a teenager, this practice of pushing it all down was so habituated that when my parents announced they would be divorcing, I followed their example by barely reacting. I put on my tough-girl shield and pretended like it didn't matter, allowing their news to slide off of me like I was Teflon.

The Reset Button

Their pronouncement wasn't a shock either. Kids always know more than we give them credit for. At that point, I was fifteen, and we were living in a wealthier neighborhood about twenty minutes away from our trailer home. We had moved there when I was thirteen, a shift from rural living to a middle-class suburban enclave, where neighbors were mere feet away instead of acres. The area was in the same school district, but the vibe was decidedly more upscale. Family was still close though—my dad's sister and her kids were right around the corner.

From my perspective, the move was awesome. There was a group of studious "good" kids close by that helped keep me on track, and my cousin and his friends were the perfect playmates whenever I wanted to blow off some teenage steam. Though I was only thirteen and in middle school, whereas he and his friends were juniors, I welcomed myself into their group and they didn't give me any pushback. I fancied myself old for my age and I was pretty eager to run with the cool crowd. My parents allowed it because I was with my cousin. They assumed he was "watching" me, even though he was also letting me party and drink with him and his buddies.

My parents had opposite reactions when it came to living in our new neighborhood. By my dad's standards, we'd made it. It was a bigger, nicer house, in a good area—hell, he even had a neighbor who was often ready with a beer for him at the end of his workday. I think my dad felt that kind of satisfaction we all long for. That feeling of "That's it. Finally. Now I can relax." My mom, on the other hand, did not seem as content. She had taken on a new sales job that required her to travel, so she was getting to see other parts of the country. She was having fancy dinners with clients and meeting all sorts of different people. Her world was getting bigger, while my dad's was staying the same size.

The separation happened about a year or so after we had moved into our new home. I had gleaned they were having problems, overheard some heated exchanges and minor arguments here and there. But my understanding that they were truly having issues came when I returned home one night and found my dad cleaning up broken glass. When I asked him what happened, he grunted out something like "Ask your mom," which is how I knew that I had walked into the aftermath of a terrible argument. My reaction? That there was nothing to see here—I told myself my parents were ridiculous, rolled my eyes, and walked out. Underneath that, though, was the shock I felt at seeing such a chaotic scene. They'd never behaved that way before—but my emotional reaction stopped there. I didn't allow myself to imagine the details of how the room had gotten that way. I never talked to my mom about it either. Instead, I pushed past it and told myself it didn't matter.

Over time, I came to realize that my mom had been having an affair. I can't remember how I found out. I must have overheard an argument at some point because I don't recall anyone sitting me down and explaining what had happened so that I might be able to understand that their marriage had been deteriorating for a while. If they did, I blocked it out or was too busy to notice—or too tough to let on that I cared. At the time, all I saw was the "final event." I took my mom's actions as a betrayal. I felt loyal to my dad and thought what she did was unforgivable.

Marriage and motherhood came early for my mom. My parents got together in high school and she had me at twenty. She never really had time to "be" or "become" without the restraints of a husband and family. Of course, that's how I understand things now when I look back at what she did—but back then, at the age of fifteen, all I understood was that she had chosen someone else over me and my dad. So when it came time to choose who to live with, I chose my dad.

My mom moved out and life completely changed.

At the time of their divorce, I had sufficiently established myself as head partyer among my large group of friends. I was drinking, smoking, and dabbling with pot and the occasional pill by freshman year. So by the time my family broke up, I had plenty of avenues for escape. I assumed I was being stealthy and that I was successfully avoiding getting caught blind-drunk or high. The truth is probably more that my parents were overwhelmed by the breakdown of their marriage and focused on rebuilding themselves, which made it hard for them to notice all that was happening with me. Also, as much as I partied, from the looks of things, I was acing life. And actually, now that I think about it, this was probably the first time I successfully pretended to be perfect. Cameo the Perfect Kid. Working, competing in sports and music, earning great grades, maintaining a busy social life… the "proof" of my perfection was all there. And my parents bought it. They accepted my 'good kid' performance, maybe hoping what they *had* noticed wasn't as bad as it seemed, and left me to my own devices.

As I said earlier, I never doubted that my parents loved and supported me. But my relationship with them was never warm and squishy. I never shared any of the typical teenage drama that was going on with me or my friends. And I certainly never talked to them about how I felt about their divorce. They were authority figures, not confidants. My partying and my deepest feelings were always kept out of view.

That became even more true once my mom moved out. Suddenly, my parents had other things going on. My mom started dating a lot, which made her less available to me. Once a constant presence at nearly every one of my after-school events, it seemed that I now had to compete with her work, her travel schedule for her job, and her social calendar. Though it was just a few times, I can distinctly remember instances where she was only there for five minutes. It likely stood out for me because it was so different from the previous years when my parents sat in the stands as a unit. As for my dad, he maintained his involvement in all of my activities, but until he met and married my stepmom a few years later, his sadness and loneliness was undeniable.

My parents were in their mid-thirties and starting new lives. Two humans who in my eyes were always just mom and dad were now behaving like actual people. By which I mean, for the first time, they had an existence outside of their work and... me. And that was very different.

But I was *fine*.

My parents' divorce coincided with the start of my first real relationship. We'll call the guy I was dating Bob. He was the picture-perfect boyfriend: homecoming king, a good student, a star athlete, dreamy, and so very sweet. I was a sophomore; he was a senior. We went to different high schools and met through mutual friends. We hit it off immediately. Bob coming into my life at that point did more than just distract me from what was going on at home: It showed me the possibilities of what a family could be. Whereas my family had begun living like three separate entities, Bob's was a single, solid unit. His parents were always around and involved. They all really *talked* to each other and had extended family holiday and birthday parties where everyone was included. It was like living inside of a Hallmark movie. Though I still considered myself a lone wolf, I preferred to be alone at Bob's house than my own. In fact, I often hung out there even when Bob was busy doing something else. His parents allowed it. I think they understood I needed to be there.

He and I were not only boyfriend and girlfriend, we were also best friends. He was my perfect counterpart. Bob was reserved; I was a wild child. He was the peacemaker; I was the drama queen. We rarely argued—mostly because he went along with whatever I wanted. I had a voice in our relationship in a way I no longer really had at home. I still never confided in him about my feelings over my parents' divorce, however. Feelings were messy and uncomfortable. How could I be the life of the party if I was weeping in a corner about something I couldn't change anyway? What would even be the point? So while I savored the comfort that he and his family provided, I never let the well of tumult I was feeling at the time spill over.

Bob and I stayed together even after he went off to college an hour and a half away. We spent most weekends with each other. After working my ass off during the week at school, I would either stay with him in his dorm room or spend the weekend with him at his home. Somehow, my parents allowed it. I either put up such a fuss that they relented, or they were comfortable enough with me going that they didn't worry about saying no. They liked Bob as well, so I think they told themselves that he would take care of me and I would be safe. Little did they know that I was spending my weekends shooting tequila shots until I was blackout drunk. As long as I was making it to school on Monday morning, they didn't say a word about what I did on the weekends. And in fairness to them, I maintained a 4.0 GPA, so there were few signs of my debauchery. I should be clear though, the pressure to be at the top of my class was something I put on myself. For me, it was a point of pride.

With all the time I spent with Bob at college, I was more than ready to put my high school career behind me—so much so that I decided to leave school early. In fact, I had enough credits to graduate when I was a junior, but I decided to stay through the volleyball season of senior year. By January, I'd left high school and enrolled in a postsecondary program at the local university.

I felt so done with high school and was anxious to start the next thing—which, for me, was college. I thought I might eventually go to law school, so I was eyeing the path it would take to get there. Mostly, though, I just wanted to move forward and take on the next challenge. So five days a week I would drive the half hour to my classes in the morning and in the evenings;

meanwhile, I worked as a receptionist at the radiology department in a local hospital.

I was doing all of the things I was told I *should* be doing. According to my mental right-thing/wrong-thing meter, I was well into the right-thing. Whether I was happy or satisfied is a whole other question. One that it never occurred to me to ask myself. I was just too focused on working toward the goal of joining Bob at his university. But I did have other options.

I loved playing volleyball. As I said, it's the reason I stayed in high school for the fall term of my senior year. The sport tapped into my drive to compete and excel. I even won a number of local and district awards, which opened doors to play at the collegiate level. I passed them up, however. I didn't want the demands and expectations that would come with college athletics. After pushing myself so hard in high school, I was drawn to the prospect of little responsibility and the guarantee of a lot of fun.

By the time I finally enrolled in college to join Bob and our friends, I had enough credits to be considered a sophomore, even though I was a freshman on campus. During the next year and a half, I alternated between attending class and soaking myself in alcohol at parties. I lived off-campus at one point and my apartment became the pre-party hub, where we could get hydrated and pregame before heading out to whatever bar. I waited tables, got solid grades, and buried myself in the social scene. By that time, Bob and I were at the on-again, off-again stage of our relationship. I think we both knew it was time to move on, but being without each other felt so strange and foreign that our breakups never lasted very long.

Somewhere along the way, my desire to go to law school dissolved. In fact, my interest in college as a whole started to fall flat. The constant cycle of class, work, and parties felt more like a grind than a life. I got itchy for the next thing, the next step, the next whatever. I no longer knew why I was there. What was it all for?

The Reset Button

There had to be more to the world, I told myself. The thought that life added up to high school, college, a job, and then moving back to your hometown to start a family felt confining. I didn't know what I wanted, but I was feeling sure that college wasn't it. The fall of my sophomore year I flew to New York to visit a friend. I was wondering if maybe the city was what I was searching for. While there, my friend and I went to this little café to have lunch. As we ate, we noticed a group of guys walk in. They were clad in leather and utterly cool. "They must be in a band," my friend said. I looked over and noticed one guy in particular.

It was Greg.

Before Greg and I officially became a couple we had crossed paths a number of times. Life seemed to keep plunking us into the same place until we finally got the message from all the serendipity. The first time we met we didn't really meet at all. My dad had heard Greg's band perform at our town's bar and thought they were great. So I hired them to play at my prom. Then, the January of my first year at university, his band played at a place just off campus. I remember watching him later that night at an after-party, wondering who this guy was fiddling with his acoustic guitar. We ran in similar circles, so we met and chatted a bit. A few months later, when Bob and I were in the middle of one of our many breakups, Greg took me to see the band Leo in concert in Columbus. But none of those meetings ever really led to much of anything.

So there we were, both hundreds of miles away from home in a random café in New York City, staring at each other. He was with a new band. They were on tour and opening for Shakira. He was there to perform in Madison Square Garden. Madison Square Garden! It was amazing. It turned out that he was offered the chance to audition for this new group that had a record deal and everything. Now he was playing arenas. Though it meant leaving his brother, best friend, and other bandmates, Greg was driven to succeed and couldn't pass up the opportunity. I was in awe. More than that, though, I was inspired. I thought: I could do more too.

I finished out the fall semester at school, but my heart was no longer in it. Greg and I kept in touch, but nothing romantic happened. Over spring break, I went to his album release party to celebrate with him. When I got back to my apartment at school, I discovered the aquarium that I'd had from childhood was completely shattered. My roommate's boyfriend had gotten angry and smashed it. That was the final straw for me. My college life was in literal and metaphorical pieces. I was tired of living the life that I was told I should be living. It might have completely thrown my right-thing/wrong-thing meter off, but I couldn't be there anymore. I had no direction and no idea of what I wanted for my future. The only thing I did know was that there had to be more out there in the world than a degree and a job. To my dad's dismay, I quit school with no intention of returning. I needed time to figure myself out.

I moved in with my mom. She was living in Columbus, which was an hour or two away from my hometown and school. Though Bob and I were still on-again, off-again, my move to the city created distance between us and led to a permanent fizzling out of our relationship. At that point, it was clear that he and I wanted different things. Bob was secure in his choices of getting a degree and staying near home to build a life for himself there. All I knew, however, was that those choices were precisely what I didn't want. My mom was happy to have me as well. Although we never discussed anything outright, she and I had gotten to a really nice place in our relationship. She did make sure I contributed to the bills a little, mostly so that I had to get a job instead of dwelling on my confusion.

Several months later, I discovered that Greg, too, was living in Columbus. His band had been dropped by the record label due to poor album sales, and he was sleeping on a friend's couch until he fully figured out next steps. But Greg, being Greg, didn't let the setback bring him down. Though he was single when we reconnected at this point, it took a while for Bob and me to officially end things. So Greg and I hung out as friends until the point where we were both single. But even before we started dating, I was drawn in by Greg's drive. His appetite for living a big life was infectious. He got a job working in sales, which, for a guy who loves performing, was perfect. The commission pay structure meant that his salary would only be limited by his ability, which really appealed to his tenacious personality. For most people, going from being a rock star to being a salesman might make them feel like their life is over. Not for Greg. He just put that same full-throttle energy into being the best damn salesman he could. He was unstoppable, and I knew I wanted to be along for the ride.

RESETTING YOURSELF

Blinking Into Marriage and Motherhood

Adulthood. I felt like I had it down. Giddy with happiness, I was a twenty-one-year-old with a budding career in sales for a life insurance company and a fantastic boyfriend. Outside of work, Greg and I had the money and freedom to come and go as we pleased. We were chomping at the bit for all of the opportunities the world had to offer. Life was a seduction of possibility and we were there for all of it.

For about a year.

Those first twelve months with Greg were heady in the best sense. Our relationship came at the perfect time—we were each coming off of breakups and nursing a failed pursuit. For me it was college. For Greg, it was losing his record deal. Maybe that was why we finally committed to each other after doing those tentative dances all of those previous times. I think we were both ready for something solid to hold on to.

For me, dropping out of college wasn't as much of an answer as it was an exciting road into the unknown. I'd anticipated the search for an answer, but what I hadn't guessed was that I would have a champion and partner alongside me on my journey. With both of us venturing into the corporate world, it was only natural that we leaned on one another for support.

Eventually, I began working as a financial advisor at a Fortune 100 firm. Yes, I was a twenty-one-year-old financial advisor. What I didn't have in life experience I made up for in studiousness and enthusiasm. I obtained all of my professional licenses and had a renewed thirst for knowledge, one that I had lost in my mundane college classes. Greg had transitioned into the mortgage industry by that time, so in addition to the financial regulation studies we were both required to do for work, he and I listened to audiobook after audiobook on our way into work. The subject of each? Crushing it in the business world. We were constantly pushing one another to grow and fed off of each other's desire to walk boldly through life. In Greg, I had found someone who shared the same philosophy—that the world was out there for the taking. In me, Greg had discovered passion and my "let's go for it" attitude. We shared a competitive spirit and found comfort in jobs that offered commissions. It tapped into our drive to get better and better, to earn more and more.

Our life felt electric and I was wholly smitten with this wonderful man. I relished the fact that I was with someone who had already achieved something. And not just a little something. He'd fulfilled that faraway dream that just about every teenager with a guitar longs for—playing amphitheaters and arenas before a roaring, cheering crowd. He had proof that he wasn't all talk. And, for me, that meant everything.

The determination and grit Greg and I shared wasn't reserved for just our careers. Whatever energy we put in during the day was matched by our enthusiasm for nightlife. When Greg had a gig, I'd go along with him as his personal groupie. We'd stay out all night and party like rock stars. Even when we planned to stay in for the evening, we'd sometimes stop off at a local bar and down four shots each just to get a quick buzz before heading home. Greg was the ideal match for my social hunger.

On nights out I transformed from Cameo the Career Woman into Cameo the Partyer. I was the woman who could be counted on to convince the early nighters to stay for "just one more drink," which inevitably turned into five. And Greg, for his part, would be giving that extra nudge to keep the festivities going. We were each other's party-wingmen, and we reveled in it.

But as much as Greg and I were similar, our approach with people and situations was often different. I was the type of person who came up with an idea and immediately threw myself into it. Picture the old cartoons where someone shoots themselves out of a cannon—that was me, gripping tightly onto whatever idea I had in the moment and lighting a fire under myself until I was airborne. Greg was more reserved in his pursuits. He was just as committed but more thoughtful and calculated in his approach. When it came to me, his first instinct was always to support whatever endeavor I was hurling myself toward. He managed to be my champion while also providing me with a mature analysis of any potential consequences. This was especially so when my Big Ideas occurred while I was drinking. Under the influence, I could often mistake something reckless for something that was totally reasonable. It's not that I sought out danger; it's more that I was kind of innocently oblivious. Frankly, I was also a bulldozer who flattened whatever was in the pathway of my objective. Greg didn't share this same recklessness when he was drinking. That, or he just passed out before he got too rambunctious. For me though, he remained my champion no matter the circumstances (or the number of adult beverages involved)—even when he had an inkling that I wasn't making the best choice. There he'd be, right next to me, subtly guiding me along, protecting me from whatever my blinders were preventing me from seeing. He was more sensible, as sensible as a person can be while still appreciating a good party and drinking folks under the table. It was less that he tried to talk me out of bad situations than that he would metaphorically wrap me up in bubble wrap so that my poor choices wouldn't have lasting effects.

I can still vividly remember one such "bubble wrap" instance. Greg and I were taking our first big vacation together at an all-inclusive resort in Jamaica. One afternoon, there we were, drunk and hungry and not able to eat because everything at the hotel had shut down until dinner. I was single-minded in satisfying my appetite, however. The ticker tape in my brain was blank but for Must. Get. Snacks. Now. So we took a taxi to a small market in town. I proceeded to waltz (or zigzag) into the store, eagle-eyed for some Cool Ranch Doritos and Raisinets. I barely noticed the group of men hanging out by the entrance. With my mind filled up by thoughts of processed foods and sugar, I failed to notice Greg's silent angst until we got to the cashier. After we paid, he hustled me out of the store and put me into the cab. In the rush, I realized I'd forgotten something vitally important—Sour Patch Kids (don't judge me!)—and tried to go back into the store. He refused to let me go and directed the cab to take us back to the hotel. Only later did I find out the reason for his agitation. Among some of the locals were a few men with legit machetes closely monitoring the comings and goings of the people at the market to make sure nobody was shoplifting.

Whoops!

I'd like to blame low blood sugar for my inability to notice people carrying deadly weapons mere feet from my person, but it's more likely that it was my own innocent oblivion that kept me from noticing the danger. I had a single mission: to get snacks. And, that afternoon, if something didn't have the Doritos logo, I didn't see it. But there was Greg, accompanying me into (and out of) the market, making sure that I got what I wanted but was also kept safe from being at the mercy of a machete.

All this to say that, generally, life was good. Greg and I were balancing our similarities and differences with ease. I knew early on that he would be my life partner. It may sound hokey, but we were best friends who did everything together and thought that anything was possible. I was marinating in this enigmatically beautiful combination of emotions—bliss, strength, love, stability, and more. I couldn't imagine ever wanting it to end. Neither could he. So with each of us employed at well-paying jobs, we decided to get our own apartment and move in together. He was still sleeping on his friend's couch and I was still living with my mom. It seemed only natural that we take the next step both financially and in our relationship. We were moving forward, together.

And soon after, in all that bliss, life happened. I became pregnant.

Cue the sound of a record screeching to a halt.

As it turns out, drunken partying and inconsistent birth control practices do not mix well. Just the fact that I was surprised that I got pregnant in the first place is a bit of a wonder. However, as stunned as both Greg and I were, neither of us looked at it with dread. Shock, yes. Apprehension, for sure. But never dread. We knew we would eventually be getting married, so we just decided to do things out of order. Blaze our own Cameo and Greg trail.

But, truthfully, the change was abrupt—especially for me.

As excited as I was to have a child with Greg, motherhood was not something that anyone who knew me assumed I would aspire to. I was the person who loved being an only child. I savored being in charge of myself and only myself. To be honest, before getting pregnant, it wasn't so much that I didn't want to have kids as that I didn't give it much thought. I was only twenty-two and assumed I had many years before I had to seriously think about my reproductive choices.

Here I was in a year-old relationship, having just moved in with Greg, and trying to get my career off the ground. Now suddenly I was also having a baby. It was as if I'd blinked and found myself in a completely new identity. I couldn't drink. I couldn't stay out all night—nor did I have the energy to—and my fit body was expanding in ways I had no control over. The changes required were swift and sweeping. My emotions jumped between excitement over the leap into motherhood and a kind of dumbfoundedness over all of the adjustments I was making. Whether I liked it or not, I was no longer a lone wolf, in body or in life. And that took some getting used to.

Greg was able to transition more easily. Let's face it, men have nine months to get used to the idea of a having a baby. To be clear, he couldn't have been more supportive—he went to every doctor's appointment and he wore his excitement about becoming a father on his sleeve—but at the end of the day, he wasn't responsible for housing another human. I didn't quite resent that difference between us, but I definitely was aware of it. Yet, I didn't share those feelings much. It just wasn't what I did. My go-to coping strategy still was to slap a smile on my face and tell everyone that everything was fine. Silver linings and all that good stuff.

So I pushed forward and decided to embrace my new identity of mother and homemaker with gusto. That's when I fell hard for Rachel Ray. She became my beacon of all things delicious and homemaker-y. Cooking, which had always fallen under my parents' perfectionistic umbrella, likely due to their busy schedule, was made to be fun. I could pinch and dab and estimate rather than measure with precision. With her help, I felt like I could crush my new role. So without looking back or allowing myself to feel all of the *things*, I cooked. I made a home. I prepared to become a mother.

Then there was my quickly shifting relationship with Greg. People refer to the first year of a relationship as the honeymoon phase. Indeed. Though Greg and I both believed we were going to be together forever, we hadn't necessarily experienced each other's "realness" yet. Unless we were under the influence, we barely argued during our first months together. How could we?

He and I were too busy immersing ourselves in our careers and partying. We were still learning those little idiosyncrasies about one another that pop up in a new relationship. What buttons get pushed when? What triggers this person? Why do they do the dishes that way? How will they relate to your family? How do they relate to you? But then impending parenthood came. Greater weight and meaning were put on everything between us. We were no longer the fancy-free couple that doubled as the party's welcoming committee. We still went out, but barely. We bought a home and were suddenly homebodies—and not the kind that stops off at the bar to suck back some shots beforehand. We played video games. We cooked. We were... different. This turn of events required us to experience a crash course on each other and this new way of life. But if we didn't like it, we had no tools or history to lean on in terms of how to deal with it.

Then beautiful Faith was born.

And just like that, I was a mother. And that felt wonderful and right. For the first time, I understood what unconditional love meant. I experienced this beautiful combination of feeling both important and humbled by her. Whatever life transitions I barreled toward without processing, being Faith's mother never felt wrong.

For both financial reasons and the sake of my own professional goals, I decided to go back to work after my maternity leave ended. I had started at a new bank while I was pregnant and was still proving myself to the company. Greg's mom, who lived about a half hour away, agreed to take care of Faith for us during the day.

I could not have been more grateful to Greg's mother for caring for Faith on those days that he and I worked. She was (and is) a very loving grandmother and it put me at ease knowing I was leaving my three-month-old with a member of our family. However, as most mothers (and fathers) probably know, that gratitude came with a big but... To be honest, my mother-in-law could have been the real-life embodiment of Mary Poppins and I still would have had a hard time. If you haven't realized it already, I'm someone who likes to take control of things. So you can imagine the challenge it was for me to take what had become the most important thing in my life—Faith—and cede control over her while I was at work.

Complicating matters was that my relationship with Greg's parents was still new. I was welcomed into his family, but they were very different from my own. It wasn't anything bad or good—it was just different. And when Greg was around his family, I felt like he was different too. It was a kind of culture shock I'd never had to deal with before. The last time I'd become a part of a boyfriend's family was in high school. Not only was I just a kid, but things at home were in tumult. This time around, as an adult, I wasn't seeking the same security I needed back then. I was happy with our little duo (and now trio) as it was. I also hadn't realized how ingrained in me my own family's culture and practices were. My dad's fastidiousness. My mom's uncompromising cleaning schedule. The fact that there was a distinct place for every little thing in our house—from the mail to a mere paper clip. And, of course, there was my family's shared appreciation for each other's sense of independence.

For me, there wasn't just one way to do things: There was an *only* way.

Greg, on the other hand, had grown up with his brother on a farm. His mother, a retired art teacher, sees potential projects in everything. Her creativity and talent enable her to envision the possibility in just about any textile you might come across. A toilet paper roll can be made beautiful. A discarded bottle cap can become a part of a larger work of art. It's incredible. It also means, however, that their house is filled with projects in varying states of progress. In Greg's family, self-expression has always trumped pristine perfection. I also wasn't used to what was probably the normal ribbing between siblings and the specific role each child plays within their family, even as adults. As an only child, this dynamic was utterly foreign to me. So was the fact that Greg reverted back to his familiar family role of jester when we all got together.

All of this newness came on the heels of Greg's mom becoming our full-time childcare provider. So it was definitely another learning curve for me. I didn't know where the boundaries were. Even when I did, I didn't know how to communicate them thoughtfully. Everything from when Faith napped to what she ate felt like a minefield. My gratitude was waging an epic battle with my need to control things. The result was either me pushing my feelings down and saying nothing, me complaining to Greg privately and feeling annoyed when he would do nothing, or me blurting out my unhappiness in a way that was probably hurtful to my mother-in-law.

Graceful expression was not a strength of mine. As much as I considered myself a social butterfly, I was also never one to spare someone's feelings. I was honest—sometimes to a fault. In my lone-wolf mind, I wanted what I wanted, thought what I thought, and that was that. But there were repercussions. I remember when my sister-in-law was getting married to Greg's brother. Even though I was very new to the family and we didn't know each other well, she asked me to be a bridesmaid. It was her wonderful way of welcoming me into the fold. I was pregnant with Faith at the time, but I had also never been a bridesmaid before and agreed to participate. Well, the wedding day came and there I was, eight months pregnant wearing an eggplant-colored dress. I looked like an actual eggplant and said as much out loud while laughing about my bloated appearance. Then, as all of the bridesmaids were helping my sister-in-law with last minute touch-ups and putting on our matching necklaces (a gift from the bride, no less), I proceeded to huff and blurt out something along the lines of "I would never put anyone through all of this!" Talk about a cringe-worthy moment. But that was how I felt and, back then, I couldn't see why I shouldn't be able to share it. That was just how I operated. It was a constant toggle between crushing honesty or a tense silence.

I'm sure my mother-in-law has many stories that she could share about times when I failed to consider her feelings or gave her the cold shoulder while I was struggling to manage my inner tornado of emotions. Sadness and frustration about all that I was missing with Faith, the fact that my mother-in-law didn't always do *exactly* the things I asked her to do in the *way* I asked her to do them, feeling like Greg wasn't always supporting my feelings—I was at the end of my rope and all it took was a single blanket to toss me over the edge.

Managing my anxiety over whether I was getting enough bonding time with Faith was a daily challenge. In researching ways to bond, I discovered that some people sleep with a blanket or a piece of clothing and then give it to their baby while they're away. The premise is that your scent is there with your child, even when you're not. I loved this idea. So I slept with a particular blanket and instructed my mother-in-law to put it in Faith's crib while she napped. It gave me some solace to know that Faith would, at least, have a small part of me with her while I was at work. That night when I got home, the blanket that I'd left for her was lying on the living room floor, and there was Faith, sleeping in her crib and cuddling with—my mother-in-law's shirt. Now, there are so many legitimate reasons why and how this could have happened, but I could hear *none of them*. I was frozen with confusion and rage.

What. The. Fuck!

Greg saw a side of me that night that he had rarely, if ever, seen before. He was familiar with my anger—he'd seen that before—but he'd never seen me overwhelmed and crying. Once we finally had time to speak about the situation privately, my deep freeze of shock began melting into hot tears. He wasn't used to seeing me like that and immediately understood the severity of how upset I was.

Not long after that night, we decided that I would stay home with Faith. It was just too hard and complicated for me at that point to manage having a family member as a caretaker. The only other option would have been to send Faith to daycare, and neither of us were ready to do that yet. And thankfully, Greg was making enough money at that point for us to be able to afford for me to step out of the workforce for a while.

My life had taken a series of hard lefts after those first twelve months with Greg. Though he was making lefts as well, from my perspective, they were softer and more curved. He could still inhabit the person he was pre-fatherhood. While Faith was still a baby, there were occasions when he'd go away for the weekend to play with his band and hang out. Other times, he would spend his free time with friends playing video games. These were all friends that I knew as well, but I was never invited. It didn't occur to Greg that I too loved video games or that I loved and could play music also. In my head, I understood that he was just craving separate bonding time with his buddies—*totally normal*—but it was a craving I was not at all familiar with. I had lots of friends but very few good ones. For me, Greg was my best friend. He was the person I wanted to regularly bond and pal around with. His need to do that with other people made me insecure. It felt like a kind of rejection. When he planned those weekends and nights out it was never discussed or debated beforehand with me; he just made the plans, told me, and went through with them. The assumption was that I would be home to take care of Faith.

Sure, if I threw a huge fit he'd agree to stay home, but that choice would only be in reaction to his controlling wife. Both options left me feeling frustrated and like I didn't have a voice.

Greg even went on tour for six weeks with another band at one point. Faith was two at the time. I was so thrilled for him! It was a wonderful opportunity for him to take time to focus solely on his passion. That persistent need I had to push through things and see a silver lining overtook any negative feelings I had about Greg's outside commitments. I didn't want to admit that I could feel rejected or lonely or jealous of Greg's other loves.

We continued to see Greg's family pretty regularly, which also caused tension between us. It wasn't that his family wasn't supportive; it was that I felt distant from the Greg I knew when we were around them. He transformed from this fun-loving thoughtful person to this loud, ridiculous guy who never wanted to rock the boat. If we made a decision or commitment to do something in particular or to parent in a certain specific way or to do something that maybe was different from how his family would do it, it would often fall by the wayside the minute his parents or brother challenged Greg about it. This left me feeling like I needed to guard our decisions closely and fight for them on my own—which, in turn, gave the impression that I was some domineering, controlling bitch-wife. As if Greg could barely go to the bathroom without my approval. What were probably meant as innocent jokes about me being "the boss" soon became regular schtick. Rather than correct the record, Greg yucked it up along with everyone else. I started feeling like a cartoon and punch line more than I felt like a member of the family. And the more the cracks about me were made, the more I inevitably dug in with Greg behind the scenes. It was a self-fulfilling cycle that left me feeling like an "other" when I was with both Greg and his family. I just couldn't understand why he wouldn't step out of his comfort zone and stick up for me.

I told myself I was happy. And truthfully, I really was most of the time. But I also felt like a walking contradiction. I loved working and building a career. I loved being home with Faith. I loved our little family. I loved my alone time. I felt loved by Greg. I felt rejected by Greg. It was so much back and forth—like I was playing my own mental tennis match. There was no way I could express it to Greg with any clarity. Looking back now, this was probably the start of me losing myself. Little by little, who I was gave way to who I needed to be in any singular moment. The loss began so gradually that I couldn't even pinpoint those moments on a timeline if I tried. But cell by cell, I began very slowly disappearing.

RESETTING YOURSELF

Losing My Identity

The author Gretchen Rubin coined the phrase "The days are long, but the years are short," and I have found this to be true. Especially when children are involved. So you'll forgive me when I fast-forward. I've symbolically pushed the "FF" button on Faith's baby years, not because there weren't notably wonderful moments or countless blissful firsts with a new baby and not because there weren't extremely challenging moments as well. Yes, there were arguments between Greg and me. Yes, Faith had tantrums and sleepless nights and challenging episodes. And yes, I had moments (if I'm honest, more than moments) where I felt lost or underserved or overworked or generally disgruntled.

I know I previously admitted that it was around the time of Faith's infancy that I began to feel as though life was chipping away at me, that I was starting to disappear. And that's true. But it's also true that I had no freaking clue it was happening. Even now, when I look back at those long days and short years, I recall feeling (mostly) happy. When you're hip-deep in ordinariness and focused on survival, it's hard to pinpoint those moments where flecks of who you are vanish like so many dead skin cells. Once Greg and I decided that I would stay home with Faith, we fell into such a steady groove of living that the tiny compromises and shifts in who I was occurred so gradually that I barely realized they were happening.

I returned to the workforce when Faith was three and old enough to attend preschool. Greg and I both had the opportunity to transfer to positions in our town's local bank branch. He was still working in the mortgage department and I was still a financial advisor, and we were five minutes away from Faith. It was an ideal situation.

It was around this time that we started talking about baby number two. Being Faith's mom had transformed my understanding of what I wanted. As I said, before I became pregnant with her, I wasn't even sure I was ever going to have children. But now that I had her, I realized that motherhood helped complete me emotionally in a way that I never imagined possible. How could I not want to have that experience again? Greg and I also wanted to give Faith a sibling. She was already almost four, so we figured we needed to start trying if we wanted them to be anywhere close in age. Since the first pregnancy came as a surprise, we had no sense of how quickly I could even get pregnant. Well, it didn't take long. It felt as if a minute later, I was pregnant with Ben.

Since I pretty much collided with pregnancy on the first go-around, I figured this second one was my chance to really look after myself through diet and self-care. It's not that I wasn't mindful of those things with Faith, but this time I was more mature, my life was more established, and I could really nurture myself in a way that I wasn't prepared to do with my first baby. I felt great and it was a really happy time. Greg felt it too. In fact, one morning, during our short commute into work, he turned to me and said serenely, "I just feel like everything is so perfect."

And that's the day I went into labor, sixteen weeks early.

It's important to note here that although part of my commitment to self-care included reading about pregnancy milestones and such, I conveniently skipped the chapters about preterm labor. I assumed I would never need to know what was held in those pages. After all, I felt amazing and there was no way something like that would ever happen to me. So that day, when I found myself going from feeling a bit weird to feeling full-on contractions, I had absolutely no idea what to think.

I still haven't forgotten the look on my doctor's face when he examined me that morning. I'll also never forget the feeling in the room, an anxious tension that was so palpable I knew things were bad before the doctor uttered even one word. Essentially, we were told that I would either be giving birth that day (which would be extremely risky for the baby) or I would need to spend the next four months in the hospital on bed rest. Giving birth to a twenty-four-week-old baby was simply out of the question, so Greg and I prepared ourselves for a long haul in the hospital—as if it was our decision to make. It's incredible how your mind and heart come together to protect you from a potentially earth-shattering experience. But, like a bully, reality pushed its way in and, in the ambulance on the way to the hospital for my long stint on bed rest, I went fully into labor.

Ben was born before I was even officially admitted. About twenty medical professionals were in the room with us, and for seven whole minutes, Ben's lungs didn't inflate. It took two doses of surfactant to help open his lungs, and then, thankfully, the second intubation was successful. The first unknown hurdle, one of life or death, had been crossed.

In mere hours Greg and I went from basking in the perfection of our lives to welcoming a one-pound, six-ounce baby.

The next 120 days I experienced the push and pull of hope and grief, exhaustion and exhilaration. It seemed the cost of every victory was paid in harrowing possibilities. We lived about forty minutes away from the hospital and, as I drove there each day, often twice a day, I would steel myself, knowing that, when I walked into the NICU, anything was possible. We all think of possibility as this wonderful gift of potential, but those months with baby Ben, I sometimes felt haunted by it. His underdeveloped lungs meant weeks on a ventilator. There were brain scans, blood transfusions, countless IVs and needle sticks, investigations into why he wasn't absorbing nutrients correctly, and on and on. Good news mixed with bad like chocolate and vanilla soft-serve ice cream, where one can never fully separate from the other.

One night, at 3 AM, we were told Ben was struggling to keep his oxygen levels up and that we might want to be with him, *just in case*. In the wee hours, we watched as his oxygen levels relentlessly dipped down into the dangerous range, listened to the alarm bells, and looked on helplessly as the medical staff swiftly attended to him. But, by morning, he had miraculously stabilized.

It took three long weeks for me to be allowed to hold my child. When I finally could, I would sit in the rocking chair with Ben and cradle him to my body, skin to skin. I can still see the room so clearly in my mind. The perpetually dim lighting the hospital maintained, so as not to disturb the infants in the six isolettes. All of the accompanying machinery. And of course, the sounds. The alarms, the beeping... all of it. And there I would stay for hours, rocking with Ben, back and forth, wishing I had the power to make him well. When I wasn't with my baby, I would often be pumping breast milk so the nurses could put it in his feeding tube.

After some time in the initial NICU, Ben was transferred to a specialized respiratory NICU clinic at a nearby children's hospital, in the hopes that their expertise would help him get off of the breathing machines. When he finally transitioned off of a ventilator to a CPAP (continuous positive airway pressure) machine, he had to learn things that "normal babies" do automatically, like the big three: sucking, swallowing, and breathing simultaneously, which is needed in order to eat. This was also when we learned that the significant levels of oxygen he had received to keep him alive could affect the blood vessels in his eyes and meant that he would potentially be blind. The revelation prompted laser eye surgery when Ben was still only three pounds.

Rather than falling off the cliff of despair those three months, I kept my focus on getting information from the doctors, writing everything down, and trying to understand all of the medical terminology. I kept a journal, but almost nothing was about how I was feeling—instead, I filled the pages with stone-cold updates on Ben's health. I was on a mission to understand everything I could and do whatever I needed to do to support my baby's survival. Losing my shit would only waste time. Even when I was home, I still had to keep it all together for Faith. Greg's parents stepped up in a huge way, looking after her whenever we needed at whatever hour of the day. But seeing her, having her around, was also a form of oxygen for me, and I never wanted her to see me break down. Greg, too, was doing whatever he could to simply get through the day. He was still working and went to the hospital whenever he could, but we were living on his commissions, so he had no room to fall apart either.

And so it was. 120 days. Pumping. Rocking. Hoping. Steeling. Listening. Reading. Writing.

When we were finally allowed to bring Ben home, Greg and I were so immensely grateful. It just seemed incredible that he had made it through. He'd fought and won. He was still on supplemental oxygen, but he was home. The whole situation brought Greg and me closer. We had closed ranks, as people tend to do in high-stress situations. Now that all four of us were finally home and together, we just focused on spending time with one another. It was decided that I would continue to stay home and Greg would continue working. I was grateful we had the means that allowed me to remain home because there was no place else I wanted to be.

That first year, I put all of my effort into being the best stay-at-home parent possible for my kids. I was present and available. I cooked, cleaned, and played with gusto. Faith had started kindergarten and we were nurturing her newfound independence as an elementary school kid. Greg tried to be with us whenever he could as well; since the bank was so close by, he would often come home for lunch so he could have more family time.

As the doctors suspected, Ben's eyes were damaged as a result of his extensive use of the breathing machine, and it was determined he was legally blind. He can see, but he requires a heavy-duty prescription. Other than that, he has had no lasting health issues. How amazing is that? Life had thrown us a huge curveball, but it felt like we'd hit a home run. And Greg and I understood that other families are not always as lucky. So we immersed ourselves in gratitude.

As you've probably come to realize at this point, I handle difficult times by riding above them. I don't let myself sit in sorrow and grief and trauma. I have always told myself that there is no point in wallowing. It's better and more productive to keep moving forward. And more than anything, I was desperate to take back control. For those 120 days, I had zero control. I was at the mercy of doctors, nurses, babysitters, fate, God—whatever you want to call it. I had to cede so much ownership over my life, over my heart, that when Ben was finally home, I immediately returned to being Cameo, the Controller in Chief.

Wake up. Breakfast. Get Faith ready for school. Play, read, "teach," nurse Ben. Nap time. Clean up. Pick up Faith. Snack. Homework. Cook dinner. Eat. Clean up. Bath time. Bedtime. Watch television. Sleep.

Repeat.

As specific as my routine was, initially it didn't feel restricting. It was actually calming. Peaceful.

As time passed, and as Ben's health got better, the inflated happiness buoying me began to dissipate. On the outside, I appeared to be managing everything beautifully. I babysat for friends' kids, my house always looked tidy and clean, dinner was always prepared, and I was always put together. But the seams of my satisfaction were beginning to rip. My state of mind was shifting from its grateful high to a dimmer reality.

Contradictory emotions started ping-ponging in my mind. I felt like staying at home with the kids was exactly where I needed to be but that I also missed the independence and financial power that working provided me. I knew the kids loved having me at home, and yet my purpose sometimes felt blurry in a way it never did when I was at the office. I jumped at the opportunity to help other moms out with childcare or other neighborly favors, yet sometimes it felt like I was doing it more to perpetuate an image of perfection than anything else. And my favorite moments during the day were experiencing new milestones with Ben and hearing about Faith's day at school, yet I was usually relieved when the day was over. The technicolor of security I felt when I first decided to stay home was dulling, but still, I knew that I wasn't ready to leave the kids yet. For someone like me who bulldozes through things to make them okay, I never gave myself a moment to consider hybrid options or what it was that was specifically making me doubt my choice. I just let the growing discontent sprout and silently watered it without ever acknowledging out loud that it was even there.

Back then, I didn't have a lot of respect for the mind's need to acknowledge and process trauma. So when, during that time, my slow simmer of irritation about little things would boil over into unrelenting rage, I never considered that something more was going on. Now I realize that there was so much unprocessed glut in my brain from those scary months with Ben that I had little space left for when I felt frustrated or angry or like I didn't have control in everyday life. Once I was secure in Ben's health, it was as if all of those latent feelings began bubbling up, but I ignored them completely.

About a year after Ben came home, I was itching for something I could do just for me. I needed an outlet. I decided to run a half-marathon. Mind you, I'd never even run a 5K before, but my dad was a marathon runner, and I was always athletic, so I decided to challenge myself. I thought it could serve the dual purpose of getting me back in shape while also lifting my spirits. It felt exciting to re-engage with my inner athlete once again. A half-marathon was just lofty enough to feel like I'd have to push myself physically, yet it wouldn't negatively impact my other commitments.

This was the first time Greg saw my athletic side. We'd moved so quickly from dating to parenting that Cameo the Athlete was a completely foreign concept to him. But I loved her. She was extreme. Tough. Focused. An alpha. I wanted her back because she was also 100% mine and it brought back memories from when I was younger and unstoppable. Of course, I probably didn't verbalize this sentiment with much clarity to him, so I think in the beginning he chalked my decision up to being another one of Cameo's crazy ideas! Because of that I couldn't really blame him if he assumed I would flame out after training for only a few weeks.

But I knew there wasn't a chance I would quit.

Completing the half-marathon required all of the elements I loved: commitment, digging deep physically, planning, and scheduling. But there were also costs. Date nights that consisted of partying late and drinking were incompatible with early morning runs. Cameo the Athlete and Cameo the Wife were at odds. No matter which identity I aligned with, there was always dissatisfaction and some bitterness on both sides. I knew Greg resented when I chose workouts over him, but I began resenting his resentment. With every snarky comment he uttered, Cameo the Wife got smaller and smaller until she started feeling invisible. Cameo the Athlete, however, she was just beginning.

All of my training scratched the itch I had about needing something that was all mine. And happily, the side effect of all of the work I was putting in was the return of the body I had before my two pregnancies. Except for my flapjack breasts, that is. It seemed that no amount of training could match the effects of nursing two babies. No matter what I did my boobs were content just hanging out around my belly button and I hated them for that. So I decided to get a boob job. I had no intention of looking like a Playboy model; I just wanted them to look the way they did before motherhood. I also hoped that by remolding and enhancing my physical body, I could tug my emotional self along as well. I scheduled the surgery for after the half-marathon. I assumed the operation would be the final piece in helping me recognize that once secure and confident woman I had always understood myself to be. Which is to say, I was augmenting my breasts solely for me (though there were no arguments from Greg either!).

With the half-marathon completed and a successful boob job behind me, I was fitter than I'd been for a long while and I looked really good. And yet, it didn't bring me the security and peace that I hoped it would. My emptiness was still there, pulling at me like a temperamental child. That yearning to push limits was still there too. I began feeling antsy about how ordinary my life had become. Two kids. The suburbs. Every day the same as before... I knew I was living the American dream, but I wasn't really living *my* dream. It wasn't that I wanted something in particular, it was more that the Big Life I had imagined for myself only a few years earlier felt like it was in the rearview mirror. Back then, however, I couldn't decipher all of my emotions or verbalize my feelings. I just didn't know how. I absolutely loved my kids, my husband, our home, our neighbors, but I couldn't deny that there was this itchy part of me that kept asking, "Is this it?" The feeling recalled the memories I had of how my mom felt when my parents moved from our trailer to our home in the wealthier part of town. Her discontent made so much more sense now.

Needless to say, I was lost. So I continued looking around for ways to both find and distract myself. That's about the time I could feel my rebellion brewing.

With Faith in school and Ben allowed to be in the world more, I was able to get out and socialize. We had awesome neighbors and there were a lot of playdates that occurred with a side of cocktails. Greg and I were expanding our social circle as well. Reenter Cameo the Partyer. We would indulge in boozy, blackout-drunk Saturday nights, which were inevitably followed by hungover-and-useless-Sundays. But I was getting attention and making friends. And goodness knows I adore the spotlight. So when I wasn't in training for a specific athletic event for my inner athlete, I gave the reins over to Cameo The Partyer.

When I wasn't partying, I focused on hitting the gym for Cameo the Athlete. I started kickboxing, lifting weights, and generally working out. I couldn't bear to let go of my athletic identity just because I had achieved my half-marathon goal. The gym soon became a second home. I made friends who took me seriously as an athlete. The camaraderie I felt there was reminiscent of being on sports teams in my high school years and I loved that. Months into my time there, I even started teaching fitness classes. And the time I spent there was mine. No husband, no kids, just me. My physical transformation was noticeable too, and I enjoyed getting noticed.

The feeling of independence and new attention that I was experiencing opened the door just a crack for little misjudgments and flirtations. To be honest, I was always a flirt. I looked at it as harmless fun. And usually it was but, as I said, little rebellions were beginning.

It all began innocently enough with *him*. We'd run into each other around town and engage in a little flirty banter, but then leave it there. The evolution was slow but it was starting to turn into something that would become harder to write off. Though I was in complete denial about that fact.

My focused time in the gym continued to transform my entire physique. I was cut. My body would never have been described as dainty, and so once I put in all that effort, my muscles responded in kind. That's what led someone to suggest that I would be a good candidate for competitive bodybuilding. The idea had an almost immediate appeal to me. It was another lofty goal and one that enticed my competitive nature. It also soothed my inner teenage girl, still damaged from being teased for being so "manly." I got hooked up with a coach and made a plan to compete that next fall.

Competitive bodybuilding also drew me in because of how specialized it was. I liked striving for uncommon goals, and competitive bodybuilding was definitely a narrow field. I'd have to push my body and my lifestyle well beyond its limits, and that was intoxicating. I adjusted my schedule to meet the demands of my new commitment. Each day essentially looked like this:

Wake up at 4 AM. Teach a fitness class or train. Go home to eat. Get the kids up. Fix breakfast. Get Faith ready for school. Eat again. Head back to the gym once Greg's mom arrives to watch Ben. Run household errands. Go home to eat. Spend time with Ben. Head to Starbucks for a caffeine fix. Pick up Faith. Eat again. Give the kids a snack. Tackle homework. Clean. Cook. Eat. Clean up again. Bring Faith to evening practices. Give baths. Put the kids to bed. Run again from 9 to 10 PM. Crash with one of the kids.

Repeat.

This precise scheduling was the only way I could get through my days while still maintaining my perfectionist standards and my sense of control. And perfection and control meant everything. I still spent quality time with my kids, friends still relied on me for childcare, and my house stayed spotless with me washing my floors on my hands and knees each evening. There was no compromising and no "letting things go."

If something started to go off the rails—and let's be honest, things always went off the rails—I would lose it. It didn't matter that I oscillated between having a slow fuse and igniting quickly like a match, it always ended in a full-throttled expression of anger and anxiety. This was especially true when Greg had anything to do with the blips in the schedule—particularly when he needed something or added to my plate by simply desiring quality time with me. I expressed my irritation with abandon. I yelled. Like, really yelled. I'd let out my inner Hulk and smash something. Sometimes I'd retreat to the car and go for long drives where I could disappear and calm down.

The daily requirements of becoming a competitive bodybuilder weren't always very family friendly either. I was not only training multiple times a day, but I had to maintain a diet of six very precise meals, so indulging in a nice dinner out or some cocktails at a bar were out of the question. Late night partying was another impossibility. I also immersed myself in the bodybuilding world—researching, reading, and learning as much as I could about the sport. I was absolutely enthralled by all of it, even when I knew that it was costing me in my relationship with Greg. But I was used to being celebrated for being so driven and excelling at things. This was who I was and I wanted to give myself the chance to bask in who I was. Everyone has their personal form of therapy and training was mine. And so while I still found plenty of time for my fun, attentive, put-together mom identity, Cameo the Wife was becoming cold, distant, and perpetually pissed. I was beginning to feel like Greg was asking me to lose a part of myself in order to be his wife and I resented that greatly. Looking back,

I think it's one of the reasons I would crash with the kids most nights rather than sleep with him in our bed.

I soon began rebelling even more. That once-flirty friendship with *him* from earlier began gaining more of my attention and turned into a totally inappropriate relationship. Truthfully though, even after the affair "officially" began, it never really felt official. My thoughts didn't linger on him the way you read about in books or see in the movies. He was a distraction but I wasn't distracted by him. His attention provided me with these quick hits of dopamine that I'd enjoy in the moment and then happily go on my way. The time that we found to be together was seldom and that was okay with me. The looks and the flirty text exchanges were enough of a boost for me to deal with the emptiness I felt. And I didn't have to be anything for him. Not the best mom, the best wife, the best athlete—hell, not even the best woman. It was never serious enough for that. I could be cute and silly and fun for a few minutes and then return to a life where I felt like my sense of self was being pushed to the curb.

The guilt that I felt in the beginning of the affair was swift and sweeping, but my exceptional talent for compartmentalizing eventually took over. And the tension between Greg and me was growing. It felt as if we were at an impasse. Our ability to communicate with each other had completely dissolved and would sometimes spill into nights out with friends. We got so good at pushing each other's buttons and hitting below the belt that when a friend suggested therapy to us, we decided to give it a try.

Those first few months with our therapist were like going back to college for Relationship Communication 101. Some sessions were harder on me, some were harder on Greg, but we both felt like she was helping us actually listen to each other. It gave us both hope that maybe we could find a way back to who we were as a couple. I was relieved, because, as dissatisfied as I was, I never imagined divorcing Greg. I truly did want to figure out a way that we could more thoughtfully and honestly communicate our feelings. And yet, at the same time, I never once brought up my extramarital affair. I kept it so carefully separated from my marriage that whenever Greg and I sat with our therapist, this superfluous entanglement felt like nothing more than a distraction. It was white noise that would only serve to pull our attention away from the real problems we were having with each other. So when our therapist would point out one of Greg's shortcomings, I'd use her observations as a way to mentally validate my affair. It allowed me to bury my guilt in flimsy excuses. And, if I'm being honest, I enjoyed my little escapes, even if they were selfish, and I wasn't ready to give them up. It embarrasses me now to say, because I risked so much to do it, but I was so lost and empty that I found solace in the no-strings attention, even while I was working on my marriage.

One thing that therapy opened up for me was my sense of empathy. At some point in our sessions, Greg admitted his insecurities about my competitive bodybuilding. We were obviously emotionally and physically disconnected around this time, so the idea of watching his wife parade around in a skimpy bikini for an entire audience of people made him very uncomfortable. Of all of the reasons I'd imagined about why he was so cold when it came to my bodybuilding goals, insecurity never came to mind. I always assumed his habit of making sarcastic comments about my diet restrictions or my lack of a social life were from selfishness on his part or from a feeling that my goals weren't as important as his. It took me longer than I would like to admit to find compassion for his feelings, but I eventually did, at least somewhat. Learning that he was insecure opened my mind and my heart up to his feelings in a way that I wouldn't have been able to do on my own. Mind you, it wasn't enough for me to bail on my bodybuilding goals, but it opened the door to seeing him as human rather than as some cartoon villain.

Greg and I continued our sessions throughout the summer while I continued training for my competition in October. I worked my ass off to get ready. As a result of all the counseling, Greg made more of an effort to be supportive, which made things so much easier. And my dog-with-a-bone mentality kept me motivated and determined.

When the competition finally rolled around I really felt prepared. I was going to crush it. I was going to win. I was sure of it.

I didn't. I placed fifth.

That outcome was devastating for me. Forget the fact that I placed in the top ten in my first competition. Or that I got an award. Or that my body fat was in the single digits and I looked amazing. To me, it was a huge loss. I failed. I wondered what I'd done all of that work for if it didn't result in first place. I was used to being the best. When I set my mind on something, I was not only unstoppable, I was usually better than just about everyone else. My perfectionism and drive made sure of it. It shook my athletic identity to have worked so hard and not come out on top as I had so many times before. And if, when I wasn't being a mom or wife, I wasn't the athlete that I thought I was, then who in the hell was I?

I simply couldn't accept what I saw as a defeat. I redoubled my efforts and recommitted my mind. In the span of one year, I went from being a total novice who had never competed before to getting second place at nationals and earning my pro card. I pushed myself to the top of my game.

And that's about the time the bottom fell out of my marriage.

Greg confronted me about the affair. A friend of his had seen me out with the man I was spending time with and told him. I was caught. I was terrified. But I was relieved too.

With the revelation of the affair, my world, as I knew it, stopped. My marriage, the family life I had worked so furiously to create, was on the verge of disintegration. Why did I risk my relationship with a man I truly loved just to act like a giddy teen with someone who I had no intention of giving my future to?

I needed to understand.

As a couple, Greg and I shut everyone else out, from neighbors to good friends to family. The therapist convinced him to take some time before making any rash decisions, which I was grateful for.

Over the next few months, he and I recommitted to each other. We were beyond fragile, but we were together. We looked past drunken dates at bars to make more quality time with one another. One place we learned to connect was at the gym. He and I began working out together, which brought him into a world that I loved. It was a kind of intimacy that I really appreciated and it closed a major gap between us. And then one day while we were working out, my shoulder, which had suffered a past injury, gave out completely. Life would have to shift again.

I needed surgery on my shoulder and substantial recuperation time. That required something that I was never particularly good at: sitting still. But it gave me plenty of time to think.

I'd sit for hours in the recliner in our living room and just go over the previous year in my mind. How did I allow this to happen? Why did it feel like it snuck up on me? Why was I so angry with Greg? The therapy and forced stillness was helping me take ownership. The truth was, the real work I needed to do wasn't around my relationship. My affair wasn't really about Greg. Don't get me wrong; he and I needed help figuring out how to communicate in better, healthier ways, but I never felt unloved by him. As I said, the affair wasn't about love. It was about me. My ego. My inability to allow myself to address and feel uncomfortable feelings in a substantive way. The fact that I was ready to symbolically burn my life down for some flirty banter and a few stolen kisses had to indicate something about who I was. It had to mean that the way I was living wasn't serving me. That the rebellions I so heavily relied on for nourishment and distractions were leaving me hungrier. It turned out that I didn't just need to learn how to communicate my feelings to my husband better; I needed to learn how to communicate my feelings with myself better.

I slowly started to realize that the gradual disintegration of the person I was before I started giving myself to everyone else led me to a point I was no longer able to sustain. There was so much lying, resentment, and emptiness. For so long, I'd made choices that were about the people around me, so when I started putting myself first again, I didn't know where to focus my energy. And so it went to self-destructive, quick fixes instead of to true healing. Between my admission of the affair, my injury, and all the pain and uncertainty, I broke. The work that I had to do wasn't just about processing my guilt or proving myself to Greg. The work I had to do involved becoming a wholly integrated person.

I had to figure out how to give myself permission to step off my own personal global stage and be imperfect. That would require me to let go of all of my identities—Mom, Athlete, Wife, Controller in Chief—and come together as one fallible person.

Those long days in that chair, I often stared out the window as all of those ideas swam around in my mind. On those gray Ohio days I would think, if only I could start fresh. If only our family could start fresh. With these self-epiphanies came a yearning for a new environment, where we—where I—wasn't seeing the shadow of who I was everywhere I went.

When I shared the idea with Greg, he didn't balk. That, too, was a change. We were at a place where we could listen first before placing all of our judgments on things. What if we moved away? Started new? Went to someplace different and warm?

And that's when we landed on Florida.

The move was hard, but I knew that it was right. Without the influence and familiarity of our surroundings, our family would have the chance to rebuild on our own terms. We were barely stitched together, but we were still, thankfully, together. And Florida would also provide me with my own personal chance to begin anew. It was a clean slate for me to do the work of becoming a better, more authentic version of myself—the person I had lost. In other words, I hit the Reset Button.

RESETTING YOURSELF

Hitting the Reset Button on Ourselves

The do-over. It's so enticing. Remember how easy it was as a kid, to yell "do-over!" when something went askew—like you tripped in the middle of a game or you got interrupted or distracted? With two words you essentially erased the previous five minutes. And while I'd like to say that moving to Florida was, for my family and myself, one big life-changing mulligan, that would ignore how frayed and fragile we all were at that point. That would've let me off the hook and denied all of the heartbreak I had caused. And maybe for the first time in my life, I wholeheartedly didn't want to do that. That's why I like to call what we did Hitting the Reset Button. For me, when you reset, there's no pretending that nothing came before it. Nobody is erasing anything. It's just a way to say, let's stop, take a breath, and start again from where we are.

I would be lying if I said that I was sure the move would yield the results I wanted—a greater understanding of myself and a healthier, better-functioning family. I hoped it would, but there was certainly no guarantee. I can still recall my in-laws waving to us as we pulled out of the driveway on that hot Ohio day—me in one car with the kids snot-bubble crying, Greg in another with our cat to keep him company. As we drove out of our neighborhood for the last time, nothing more than hope and a hint of optimism kept me from calling the whole thing off.

Though moving to Florida was my idea, I wasn't trying to use our town or our life in Ohio as a scapegoat. Yes, starting fresh somewhere new, without being saddled by history or gossip, was definitely alluring. But it wasn't like moving states was magic. A clean slate is meaningless if the things that sullied it in the first place haven't been resolved. Had I not fixed my focus on reshaping my mind, my priorities, and how I communicated them, Florida would have been the sequel to Ohio, just with palm trees instead of snow.

After the move I once again threw myself into books for guidance. Just as I did at the beginning of my career, I consumed any material that I thought might help me reach my goal. The only difference was that this time I was in search of transformation and self-growth. I've always considered my books to be a set of friends. Authors like Brené Brown and Arianna Huffington were key members of my Girls Night In club, especially considering I didn't know anyone in Florida yet and my therapist was states away. Books became sage counsel that I relied upon and hung out with. And the greatest thing about reading is that you can digest it as quickly or as slowly as you want and as many times as you like. Those books helped me ask difficult questions of myself that I probably never would've thought to consider before.

As I read whatever I could get my hands on, one concept particularly hit home: the Time Management Matrix. It's a method created by author Stephen Covey to illustrate a productivity technique that helps you keep your priorities in focus at all times, even when life's little distractions pull at your attention. In this process you imagine an empty jar, some big rocks, pebbles, and sand. The jar represents your time. Your major priorities, the things most important to you in your life, are the big rocks.

The pebbles are the things that are of second-tier importance. Maybe they're things that are pressing or popular but not vital to your overall happiness or success. Then there's the sand. This represents all of the everyday distractions that (we think) demand our attention. By categorizing what's most important to you by size, it's easy to visualize where you should be placing the majority of your attention. The exercise is to ensure the big rocks fit in the jar, then the pebbles, and then the sand will filter down through whatever space remains.

This idea sparked a curiosity in me. What were my big rocks? My major priorities? And, deeper than that, what did *priorities* mean to me? As I investigated this, I realized it was about more than importance or time management. It was about *meaningfulness*. The most meaningful people and things—my husband, my children, my marriage, my authentic personal fulfillment—*those* were my big rocks. My nonnegotiables. The rocks that would dictate the amount of space left for the pebbles and sand in my jar. Back then it helped to envision this dynamic picture of a jam-packed jar filled with everything that made up my life.

Thinking about things in this way was an opportunity to take a brutally honest inventory of how I was living. It was also when it first dawned on me that some of the things I determined to be big rocks in my life weren't even in the jar at all. They were lying on the outside, pushed out by an overflow of pebbles and sand. It's no wonder I ended most days exhausted without feeling any sense of personal satisfaction or connection to the people most important to me. Like many people, I was pulled in a million different directions all the time—work, kids, marriage, friends, chores, cooking, fitness, chauffeuring, favors, last-minute problems, prior commitments, and on and on. Because I had never established my rocks, I zipped from one thing to another in a kind of simmering frenzy.

On its face, prioritizing seemed so simple, but once I dug in and looked at all of the things that were filling my jar... What. A. Shit Show! I started to recognize that many of my pebbles were included due to the influence of others. They were there as a result of my chronic case of the "shoulds." As in, this *should* be a priority for me or I can't give this up because everyone else thinks I *should* be doing it. A number of things that in Ohio I held up as vital to my contentment were actually things that were important to other people, not me. My right-thing/wrong-thing meter is one priority that comes to mind. I put so much stock and value on doing things the "right" way—such as vacuuming my floors every single day—because the necessity of doing that is what I internalized growing up. I just accepted it as a nonnegotiable part of my day. Pebbles like that took up so much space that the big rocks were pushed out. Neglected. But by reprioritizing things according to *meaningfulness*, I could ensure that I was refilling my jar based on the things that held the most value for me. And the wonderful thing about choosing these big rocks for myself was that it gave me greater ownership over my life.

These days, Greg and I have an affectionate shorthand for this process that we call Dumping Out the Jar. When the jar starts to overflow with sand—and trust me, it does—I dump it out and start again. Another way of looking at this idea is to think about it as a priority pyramid. The top of your pyramid should be the one or two things that are the most important to you. Those are the things you want to give the most time and attention to. If you're not, then it's time to dump out your jar or redraw your priority pyramid. Use whichever visual works better for you as you work this out.

Metaphorically refilling my jar or creating my pyramid also meant learning how to say no. I had to resist letting my jar fill up with sand by saying yes to things out of obligation or guilt. I had to stop people-pleasing. I had to be aware of and dismiss the "shoulds." For me to succeed in this new way of living, my decisions needed to be in alignment with the most meaningful pieces of my life, and this often made decision-making difficult, even painful sometimes. Choosing things in a more thoughtful way was foreign. I had conditioned myself to bulldoze through decisions and commitments without any analysis at all. And now I not only had to slow down and understand my choices, but I also had to reconcile the cost of them.

Decisions, choices, they all have a cost, and weighing that cost helps you gain clarity on that choice's meaningfulness. For example, when I chose to party and get drunk with Greg, the obvious cost of that was an epic hangover and a Sunday spent lying limply on the couch. In between recovery naps, I would text anyone I may have offended the night before, apologizing for anything I may have said or done that I didn't remember. I called this practice my "Sunday Sorrys." But as I ventured into what I now refer to as a Cost-Benefit Evaluation, I wanted to look deeper than glaring consequences like that.

Partying, for example, was something I always just did. It was something I had seen growing up and replicated. But now the habit needed to be considered through the lens of my metaphorical priorities jar. Where did partying fit in? Was adding yet another drunken survival story to my collection meaningful to me? Nope. In fact, none of my big rocks represented drunken socializing. So then why was it taking up so much of my time?

Looking at my choices this way clarified for me how the everyday decisions I was making, such as getting blackout drunk most weekends, were misaligned with my true priorities. It enabled me to clearly see how the cost of these late nights was much more than a throbbing headache and recovery McDonald's. It meant missing opportunities to nurture my marriage or, worse, to actually foment conflicts with Greg because of poor judgment calls I made while "Crazy Cameo" was at the helm. It also meant losing precious time to create memories with my children and went against my priority of honoring my body and mind. Above all, it meant neglecting my big rocks.

As I did this work, figuring out how to prioritize myself proved to be a more challenging feat than I imagined. As a lone wolf, only child, I probably could've held a master class on how to put myself first. However, at this point I realized that my approach to this was very short-sighted. I had to learn how to differentiate between being selfish and being self-interested. For me, being selfish means doing whatever you want, whenever you want, with no regard for anyone else's feelings, needs, or plans. Simply put, your tent consists of you and you alone. Whereas being self-interested means knowing what you want and need and then thoughtfully communicating that need to the most important people around you, without disregarding your other responsibilities. This broadens your tent to include your loved ones and the other most important aspects of your life.

How could I give myself the time and nourishment I needed for my own well-being without abandoning the other vital parts of my life or becoming the resentee? Working through giving myself permission to prioritize my own wellness continues to be a struggle that I know many of you can relate to. How often do you find yourself explaining the details of your self-care and then justifying why you deserve it?

My fitness career was one area of my life that forced me to parse out the difference between being selfish and being self-interested. Since I was carefully considering all of my choices around this time, it was only natural for me to step back from bodybuilding and consider the what and why behind my need for it. And, in the end, I realized that my pursuits were both selfish *and* self-interested.

After everything I went through when Ben was first born, the first thing I did for myself was to turn to my safe haven of athletics. I told myself that the half-marathon was *for me*.

Mine. I was mission-driven and focused on that singular goal. I think we all need that sometimes—something we can embrace as our own and feel great about giving it effort. I consider that self-interest. But here's where the slope gets slippery into selfish territory. Every choice I made at that time, from whether I chose to have date nights with Greg to if I socialized at all, was decided through the lens of crushing that half-marathon goal. While I didn't neglect my parenting responsibilities, it would be fair to say I back-burnered just about everything else. I was all about the finish line, so to speak.

The ego boost of reaching that goal led to my desire to seek out more "finish lines." To achieve the best body. To be everyone's gym bestie. To embody power. To be at the top of my game so that I could teach others. To fully embrace Cameo the Athlete and finally to win a bodybuilding competition. For me, my physical self was a vehicle to prove my worth, to be the best. And throughout my childhood and adulthood in Ohio, I used fitness objectives to harness control. By focusing only on the end result, I could suppress my problems and convince myself that I was doing everything in service of my mission, rather than as a distraction from whatever was bothering me. This escape tactic, for me, perpetuated a selfish mindset.

And yet...

Athletics has always also been a kind of therapy for me (and it still is). Working out and setting goals nourishes me; I'd be doing myself a disservice if I didn't also admit that. Even as I used fitness endeavors to avoid issues, I relied on them for calm and focus—it's been an outlet that helped center me as my life grew ever more hectic. And that aspect was me being self-interested.

And so, I'd unknowingly created this web of selfishness and self-interest that I had to untangle and understand before I was emotionally ready to dive into competition again.

After the move, I took some time to figure out how to remove the selfish, egotistical piece from competing, so I could ensure that my fitness goals wouldn't take me down a path that left no room for the other big rocks in my life. Also, practically speaking, recommitting myself to my family and marriage was my first priority, which meant I'd need more freedom over my time and lifestyle. And with things still raw between Greg and me, competing again would definitely have risked additional tension between us. Finally, I knew that finding a new, healthier mindset around my athletic goals would protect me from the spotlight, which had been so magically alluring in Ohio. The admiration I received from bodybuilding was pure ego food and I needed to figure out why. When and why did I cross the line from competing in order to pursue a healthy, individual goal to doing it for those quick hits of tantalizing adoration? Similar to how I thought about my priorities, I reevaluated for myself the meaningfulness of competition. By shining a light on how I truly felt about bodybuilding, I knew that I could one day get back into it without falling prey to my old mindset.

The process I went through around my fitness commitments is a great example of how Hitting the Reset Button helped me sift through not just what I wanted but how each want connected to every other part of my life. Through this work, all of those separate identities I'd maintained—Cameo the Mom, Cameo the Wife, Cameo the Athlete, et cetera—stopped their constant bickering for time and dominance and joined together so that I could become one holistic person. And had I not taken the time to work through this in this way, I know I would've resented taking a pause on my competition goals. I would've felt as if my independence was being threatened. But because of this process, I not only owned my decision, I felt good about it. And I knew that I wasn't saying goodbye to competing forever.

Sure enough, about a year after moving to Florida, I rejoined the competitive bodybuilding world. This time, I figured out how to incorporate the commitment into my life and not the other way around. My family was involved and it made the entire experience more fulfilling. The internal work I did after we moved also helped me learn to love the process of getting to the finish line or, in this case, the stage.

I will always love being the best. I will always savor winning. That's just who I am. But, by flipping my mental script, I figured out how to celebrate the effort instead of the result. And when I sensed I was tipping back into my old mindset, I had candid conversations with myself to get back into realignment. So even though I didn't come out on top the next time I competed, I didn't feel the despair I experienced in that first bodybuilding competition. I was proud of my progress, the focused approach, and was honored that my family, body, and mentality were strong enough to get me there. And gratefully, that ability to savor the process (as opposed to the outcome) has impacted every other part of my life.

Pressing pause on my fitness career also blocked one of my most relied upon avenues for disconnecting from my feelings. As I've mentioned, I used to push through things. Get things done. Conquer goals. My whole life up until that point was spent running, doing, moving past things. When my parents told me they were getting a divorce, I huffed and left to go party with my boyfriend. When Ben was in the NICU, my journal looked like a medical chart, sterile with stats, never allowing one emotion to make it onto the page. Even my affair was a quick fix. I wasn't cheating on Greg because I was in love, I was doing it for the fun, feel-only-the-good-things moments. I came to understand that as fit as I was, I didn't know how to live inside of my body, and I needed to explore that first in order to find some peace in my mind.

This is how I came to my meditation and yoga practice. Guided meditation and yoga helped me slow down what is often called "the monkey mind" in Buddhist teachings, allowing me to be more aware of what I was feeling. For someone like me, who chose anger instead of vulnerability, learning how to explore my emotions was quite an education. I learned how to focus on my breath so that I could tune out the mental mayhem that distracted me from understanding what I was feeling. And yoga allowed me to marinate in my own skin—to stretch and feel my body. It was so markedly different from the sensations I had when I worked out in the gym. This was more of an intentional collaboration with my body, rather than me forcing my muscles, my joints, and my heart to grind it out and surpass my limits. It gave me the opportunity to learn about myself and what I was feeling.

Mindfulness and meditation have a way of shining a light on the way you process or handle experiences. For me, issues around my ego kept coming up. I realized that even beyond my fitness practice, my ego had been dictating much of my life. So many of my decisions were made because of how they would make me look to others. I put an inordinate amount of weight on controlling people's perceptions of me—marketing an "acceptable" (read: fabulous) version of Cameo rather than the flawed real thing. We all do this to some extent, but for me, it meant that my ego was the one at the wheel. To be fair, sometimes when the ego gets involved it's there as a form of protection. Many of us, me included, feel pressure to belong, to keep up, and to get noticed. Most of us feel this pressure every day—like at school pickup, or at church, family functions, and so on. But I realized that just because your ego bullies its way in to protect you from triggers or from feeling less than, it doesn't mean it's healthy or good for your long-term well-being. It does mean, however, that it's an area that needs some attention and analysis.

For example, when we first arrived in Florida, my instinct was to dress the way I did in Ohio—to flaunt the way I looked. I wanted the attention, the gratification of being admired. Not just from men, but from women too. Don't get me wrong; I am a strong advocate of the "Look Good, Feel Good" movement, but for me, that desire was inextricably intertwined with my self-worth. I had become too reliant upon getting those looks of admiration that, at the end of the day, had no real value or importance. They were just gifts for my ego, and they weren't a true reflection of the real me. Feeding into it meant indulging habits that led to my affair and my need to feel like a rose among dandelions. So as I did all of this work on myself, I had to learn how to develop a silent ego alarm—a Check Ego Light. I'd do this by having little conversation trains with myself like:

Why do I want to wear these things? Because I want to get noticed. Why do I want to get noticed? Because I like the sense of power it gives me. But is that power real? And is that a power I'm interested in having? No. So this is my ego talking...

By having these conversation trains—and I still have them—I can deduce whether my ego is dominating my decisions (like it was in the example above). I've also realized that one of my "tells" when my ego is driving is how quickly I move to anger or resentment. As you know, my go-to emotion has always been rage, which inevitably makes everything worse. So when these charged emotions arise, I'll often summon my Check Ego Light. What I typically discover is that I was protecting myself after being triggered. Some past sadness or hurt that I'd never dealt with arose, and my ego bullied its way in to shield me.

By incorporating a regular yoga and meditation practice into my day, I ended up habituating constructive tools that I could rely on in heated moments. I learned how to be okay with feeling vulnerable and how to access other more productive emotions. More than that, I no longer feared my feelings. I learned to explore them. I acknowledged the hurt little girl who still lived inside of me from my childhood and developed a sense of compassion for myself.

Learning that self-compassion isn't weakness and vulnerability isn't dangerous opened me up to having greater compassion and empathy for others as well. It made me so much less judgmental. Understanding that everyone has a "hurt little kid" or an unresolved trauma that they are working through (or maybe still need to work though) has changed the way I connect with people. I don't just assume people are wrong or jerks or limited. Instead, I figure that like me, there's a story behind why they're reacting or behaving a particular way. We're all pulling from our own reference folder. So what is true for me may not be true for someone else.

Now I look back on how I reacted to situations in my past, and I see how I could have been more understanding or not been so quick to take things personally. When my parents divorced, I was a teenager, so all I knew and understood was that I was hurt by them. And hurt equaled angry. Hurt equaled bulldozing through things without trying to understand. That kind of defensive reaction to complex and negative emotions followed me into adulthood. As did my resentment and anger at my parents' way of handling their marriage and divorce. But now as an adult with a parallel experience to reference, I realize that they were both doing the best they could with the difficult and heavy responsibility of the decisions they had to make.

The experiences I had with my mother-in-law when Faith was a baby also come to mind. At the time, I felt I had effectively communicated my boundaries and expectations (which was nothing less than perfection and a complete adherence to my instructions). So when my mother-in-law did things differently from me, I remember feeling it was an implicit judgment on my parenting choices. Now, however, I can see that she was just nurturing and caretaking in a way that made sense to her. I'm the one who made it about me by jumping to criticism and defensiveness. As hard as it was for my ego to accept, none of her choices had anything to do with me at all. Rather than delving into all of that anger from feeling disrespected as Faith's mother, I should have spent time trying to understand why I felt so triggered in the first place. Why was I so rageful when she didn't do things my way? Figuring that out would have allowed me the opportunity to communicate with my mother-in-law in a more reasonable and substantive way. I also should have adjusted my expectations. Perfection is more than anyone can give. It's a recipe for conflict and unhappiness. Not to mention, it's unfair.

Deciding on my priorities, taking ownership of their cost, doing meditation and practicing yoga were all integral to my transformation. But things weren't perfect. I was still sometimes finding myself in a black hole of anger. There were instances where resentment would bubble up just as it had in Ohio. As you know, triggers don't go away. It's our reaction to them that changes. These days when I'm triggered, I've gotten better (not perfect!) at bringing myself back to the present moment. Instead of getting on my rage roller coaster or bottling it up until it destructively bursts out at some random moment, I've learned how to take a breath, close my eyes, stop that monkey from jumping around in my brain, and just be in the present. By bringing awareness back to what's happening right that second, I can't dwell in negativity. Rage requires your full focus. You need to stop everything and indulge in it, which is why focusing on the moment at hand can be so effective. Then, when I'm ready, I investigate my feelings (instead of indulging in them). This allows me to intelligently advocate for myself if the need arises. I use this same strategy when I'm feeling overwhelmed. After all, my life isn't any less busy than it was in Ohio. But now, because I've memorized my priority pyramid and I'm clear on which areas of my life consist of my big rocks, I'm not constantly angry anymore. So nothing has changed except for my mindset and my approach with myself.

Mindset is everything. During my life overhaul—a marriage

The Reset Button

on the brink, kids uprooted, and an intense crash course in self-improvement—it was easy to get lost in the chaos and become discouraged. My mind would run off like a freight train with cars full of what-ifs and worst-case scenarios. That's when I challenged myself to be curiously contradictory. Instead of catastrophizing, I would force myself to play out the best-case scenario in my mind. This switch in attitude and perspective turned everything on its head in the best way. Take the bodybuilding example I mentioned earlier. Instead of thinking about all that I would lose by not competing, I imagined how much time would be opened up to spend with my family. And since time with my family would help keep us together—which was a top priority—how could I resent giving bodybuilding up? When I would pull a negative experience out of my reference folder, I would ask myself what the opposite of that looked like. Then I would get in alignment with that. I also began a nighttime routine of thinking about all of the things that went right during the day and all of the things I was grateful for. This kept me from reviewing all of the day's regrets and set the tone for a more positive mindset.

Another really important component of my reset was quitting drinking. I'll talk about this more in the Deal with Your Shit section, but I don't want to ignore its impact here. For me, drinking became a life management tool that did more harm than good. It allowed me to bottle up all of my negativity rather than deal with it, "treat myself" to too many glasses of alcohol as a reward for the stress. By not drinking, I also relinquished a major scapegoat. Bad behavior could no longer be explained away by those ten tequila shots I had inhaled. And it erased those hangover Sundays, which gave me more quality time with my kids. It encouraged Greg and me to find more substantive ways to be together as well.

Hitting the Reset Button is something I do as often as I choose, and each time it gets a little easier. As new things are uncovered or difficult situations arise, I am armed with tools and trust in myself to handle it. It's a thought process that leads to a philosophy of living that brings about greater awareness, confidence, and ownership of your life. And that's made it worth the effort.

HIT THE RESET BUTTON ON YOURSELF

During the Reflection

What's your jar looking like these days?
Is it overflowing with sand? Which are your big rocks?
If the jar imagery doesn't work, then do it a different way. Write priorities down in different colors according to their level of importance. Use index cards or a journal. Remember, when you throw up your hands and lament that "that's just the way it is," you're abdicating control over your own happiness.

How exactly are you making your decisions?
If your decisions are dictated by always metaphorically turning right… maybe it's time you try turning left? Our decision processes are learned. Deciding things based on my right-thing/wrong-thing meter, for example, was a processing habit I realized I needed to break. Letting that go was one way I turned left instead of right.

Take an inventory of your relationships.
You are who you hang out with. The people who you surround yourself with, including on social media, can bring out the very best and the very worst of you. Assess how your family, friends, coworkers, and metaverse friends are influencing you. How does your interaction with them make you feel? Are they helping or hurting you? And remember, you don't owe anyone any explanations about the work you are doing. This is for you to have a better understanding of yourself.

Be open to working with experts.

Are you closed off to the idea of seeking professional expertise because of preconceived notions or stereotypes about therapy? In some circles, false narratives swirl furiously, equating professional help with weakness or of proof that something is wrong with you. But think about it; you wouldn't drive while knowing your car brakes were acting funky. So there's no reason not to seek help when you're having trouble understanding complicated feelings. The Reflection requires analysis and brutal honesty with yourself, and that can be very challenging—even scary. A counselor can help you work through those feelings as you learn to understand yourself, your mindset, and your habits better. So if you're triggered or feeling overwhelmed or anxious, do not ignore it. After all, why should your car be more deserving of attention than your mental health?

What small actions can you implement to ignite change?

Moving your physical location, like my move from Ohio to Florida, is not necessary to create lasting change. There's no reason to throw in the towel if major changes, like switching jobs or moving, are off the table. Consider whether there are micro decisions you can make. Is there a course to take? A book to read? However small, your actions will shift your thinking and help create a chain of positive change.

During the Reset

Give yourself permission to change.

You're working on bettering yourself—for yourself. Period. Stifle that nagging case of "the shoulds," along with any shame that's associated with it. Just because you were raised with certain beliefs, practices, or habits doesn't mean they are correct or serve the person you are striving to be. Let go of any sense of limitation and allow yourself to be open to new perspectives and possibilities.

Inevitably, it can feel uncomfortable or even scary when you do things differently. If and when it does, remember to stay calm. It's all worth the risk.

Open yourself up to a new center of influence.
Find new resources. Pursue books, people, classes, or other activities that are in greater alignment with who you want to be and the kind of life you want to live. Some inspiration can even come from social media, but remember to scroll mindfully. This is the perfect time for a social media audit. Curate your feed according to your mental health and your reflection work. Be aware of how posts are making you feel. Above all, unfollow anything that's triggering you. You might even want to take a social media break all together.

Start a gratitude practice.
Be thankful for what's working. Shifting your mind this way welcomes new possibilities and change. You can pray, meditate, journal, or walk in the woods… whatever you do, just take time to acknowledge what nourishes you.

You are not in control of how others act, but you are in control of how you respond.
Everyone is on their own journey. It's not your job to bring everyone along with you while you do this work. Nor are you responsible for other people's happiness. You don't have to be "right" either. Being right is relative. Conversely, when you're triggered by others, you must own your reaction.

Beware of toxic positivity.
Failure isn't an option! Feeling emotional isn't positive. Sleep is for suckers! Just keep on hustling... These ideas aren't positive; they're bullies that encourage you to push through and ignore what you're feeling. During this Reset phase, if something doesn't feel right, explore why instead of just bulldozing through it.

During the Reinvention

Creating new habits creates a ripple effect.
Change—such an uncomplicated word for something so crucial and difficult. But a thorough Reflection and Reset builds the motivation to make hard yet necessary changes, which will trickle into every other part of your life.

Hold tight to why you are doing this work.
Memorize the priorities and reasons you wrote down during your reflection period. Forget perfectionism. Prepare for some discomfort. Change feels like a new pair of shoes you haven't broken in yet. Being comfortable doesn't equal being happy, and yet it can lull us into accepting the status quo. The road to self-growth and fulfillment often requires a lot of us—unvarnished honesty, self-challenges, and hard work. I'm not promising this work will be easy, but I am telling you that it can lead to deep, profound, and lasting satisfaction.

Adjust your expectations of others.
Not everyone in your life will have the same goals, capabilities, talents, or resources that you do. By adjusting expectations accordingly, you are fostering greater understanding and empathy. It also relieves a ton of pressure as well as the potential for disappointment. Expectations are an unfair burden to place

on someone. Instead, focus on encouraging and supporting the individual to do their best. This creates an environment for happier and healthier interactions.

On the flip side, you don't have to be someone you're not for someone else's comfort. You shouldn't ever compromise who you're becoming in order to keep certain people in your life. Relationships are fluid, so sometimes stepping back from someone, even temporarily, is okay.

It makes space for people who are more in alignment with who you want to be.

Steer clear of judgment.
Judging others is the antithesis of this work. It will only cloud your thinking. Let go of the desire for something or someone to be or to react a certain way. It's a waste of your time and it will trip you up and lead you right into a negative space. A more productive question to ask yourself is whether the subject of your judgment is a good fit for who you're becoming. When you're around them, do you find it easy to follow through on the new habits you're creating or are you always falling back into your old ways? Keep your focus on the work you're doing on yourself. And if you do find yourself wearing your judgmental hat a lot, then it's time to reflect inward once again to re-center your mindset.

Growth is not linear.
You've probably already met my good friend Setback! We've all experienced them. Just when we think we're getting the hang of change, some new challenge comes along to wallop us backwards. When this happens, stay confident in all of the work you've done. Setbacks don't erase the progress you've made. In fact, they can often propel you toward a massive breakthrough. Use these tools, remember your rocks and your

priority pyramid, and keep checking in with yourself and your Check Ego Light. These habits will keep you moving forward.

Lastly, it's important to remember the tug that will likely occur between your need for agility and that innate desire to flee from the discomfort of change. As life swirls around, agility will enable you to adjust as needed, but that adjustment can make you uneasy. All of this is okay. The more you make a practice of reminding yourself that nothing is set in stone, the calmer you will stay when modifications are happening. Eventually you might even find freedom in the knowledge that if something is not working or aspects of your life change, you can change right along with them.

In all of this work, be patient, kind, and forgiving—to yourself and others. Focus on the feelings that await you on the other side of this change. Hit your Reset Button whenever you feel like it's time to go back for some reprioritization. Life moves fast and when something turns life upside down, this strategy is here, ready to help you find your way.

SECTION 2

Resetting Your Marriage or Partnership

INTRODUCTION

RESETTING YOUR MARRIAGE OR PARTNERSHIP

Initial Thoughts

I found out that a woman in my local area, whom I admire professionally and who appeared to have everything a person could ever want—a growing family, financial success, professional success, and good health—was newly single. I don't know the particulars of her situation, whether the change in her relationship status was her choice, her partner's choice, or even if it was thrust upon her due to a life event, and yet, finding out gave me pause. Although my affair was over a decade ago, every so often the reality of what *could have* happened stops me in my tracks. I am not arrogant enough to claim responsibility for the fact that Greg and I made it through that first year or so after the affair. We were running on fumes of faith in each other at that point. But I can say that once we truly bottomed out with each other, he and I finally, and mutually, made the space required for our relationship to be a part of our marriage.

That is what this section is about—learning how to use the Reset Button to open yourself up to allowing your relationship to become the third entity in your union. The Reset Button can also help you create a shared understanding of what that means, because it will be unique to every couple. In each chapter, I'll address the building blocks needed to get there: communication, commitment, and intimacy. These are fundamental to a strong relationship. When you and your partner learn together and work together, you are creating a strong foundation for a lasting and fulfilling union.

If you're able to read this section with your partner, that's great. If not, all is not lost. You can inspire change in your union even if you only start shifting things for yourself. As I've mentioned before, change doesn't happen in a vacuum, and a healthier approach to your relationship can be infectious. Remember, you can't force change on people; it almost always backfires. However, your shift can be the impetus that sparks your partner's motivation to do their own work. For example, if your approach to conflict goes from screaming and yelling to a calmer, more centered tack, your partner would be hard pressed not to notice. If you go from individual score keeping to creating shared goals, you are automatically encouraging a healthier give-and-take. That said, if you can do this with your partner, then allow this section to inspire a better understanding not just of each other but of your partnership itself.

I also want to give a quick shout-out to my single readers, my never-been-marrieds, my divorcees, my widowers. Although this section might not seem applicable to you, trust me, it still can be. If you're coming off of a divorce, these tools can provide a way to look back at where you and your partner might have gotten tripped up. If you're single, use this section to think about what a marriage or long-term partnership means to you.

Lastly, I want to be clear when I say that there are sometimes issues in a union that can't be fixed. There are also some relationships that reach a natural conclusion—no matter how much you may want it to be otherwise. There's no judgment here if that's the case. But for those of you who, like Greg and me, reached rock bottom but are now choosing to climb out of it as partners instead of as individuals—these tools can help get you there.

Here's how it all went down.

RESETTING YOUR MARRIAGE OR PARTNERSHIP

The Rockiest Bottom

Rock bottom. I thought I had been there, done that. I naively assumed Greg and I had hit our low point in Ohio. That we dove headfirst into it when we sat at our kitchen table and Greg revealed that he knew about my affair. After all, that moment led to some of the lowest points of my life—the most painful, gut-wrenching stages of grief I'd ever experienced. But no. I would find out about a year later that we could plunge even quicker and more furiously into a cavernous abyss custom-made for relationships on the brink.

However, before I get into our quick descent into the marriage depths, there is something you should know. As I mentioned in the last section, Greg and I lived very well in Ohio. Nice house. Fancy cars. New boobs. Great suburb. We looked like we had it all. What I didn't mention though, was that for the majority of that time, we were also in tremendous debt. Crushing credit card debt to be exact.

In 2006, when Faith was just about two, Greg decided to become a mortgage net branch manager. He could work from home and I could help since I was also still home at the time. We were confident in our professional acumen, had built a network, and, let's face it, were eager for the challenges and possibilities that came with being our own boss. As you know, we were dreamers, so entrepreneurship made sense. It just so happened, however, that we launched our business right around the time that the mortgage bubble burst. So while other mortgage companies were closing their doors, Greg and I, in our very driven and optimistic way, kept ours wide open. But we were struggling financially. We turned to credit cards for everything, telling ourselves that this was a valley in what would eventually lead to shining financial glory on a hill. But it didn't. This was right around the same time that Greg was invited to go on tour for six weeks. It was an opportunity he couldn't pass up, but the consequences led to an unsustainable business situation. We closed up shop. But our debt kept on growing. We did our best to manage it—transferring balances to low- or no-interest cards, figuring out payment plans—but life events (both good and challenging) would get in the way of our goals. We got married, for instance. Ben was born premature and had tremendous medical needs. I stayed home with our kids longer. So even after Greg began earning generous commissions once again, we still failed to pull ourselves out of our financial hole.

Moving expenses only darkened our financial cloud. But while Greg and I took our debt seriously, we ultimately believed that we would figure our way out of it, which is one of the reasons why neither of us considered bankruptcy as a solution. So while it was daunting at times, it never felt permanent. Our irrepressible professional optimism shielded us from feeling held back by our finances and allowed us to continue to live our lives without perseverating over our bank account. That's also why our financial situation didn't figure into our decision to move across the country. We just knew, in our guts, that we would eventually be debt free. I tell you all of this now because it's an important detail to keep in mind as I share this story.

As I mentioned in the introduction, by the time we arrived in Florida, our marriage was running on faith and fumes. As fragile as we were though, Greg and I were under the impression that we had worked out enough of our feelings that we could move forward emotionally and start anew. We weren't in denial about what happened in Ohio, but a "fresh start" mindset had taken hold and we ran with it. Or, at least, I did.

Our first week in Florida was spent moving into our rental home. Friends from Ohio came down to help us settle in, and parts of the week felt more like we were on a vacation than like we had just uprooted our lives. But then the newness wore off and things felt real. We knew no one. For the first time in our adult lives we were wholly surrounded by strangers. This was alluring and scary. I loved that we were starting in a completely different environment. New surroundings, new neighbors, no history to feel bashful about, no gossip to contend with, and the allure of fresh possibilities that come with starting over. The scary part was that we had no backup. Nothing was familiar. For a while, everything required additional work and research. We had to find our doctors, our favorite grocery store, nearby activities, and everything else that made up daily life. Any help or support we would need for the kids would have to be done by strangers. At that point Faith was eight and going into fourth grade and Ben was four and would be attending a daycare preschool. When they weren't in school, they were used to being cared for by an extended family member if neither Greg nor I were available. But now we had to rely on after-school programs and daycares—meaning we (and they) would have to put our trust in people we knew little about. This change was an adjustment for all of us. I can remember crying all the way to work after dropping Ben off at daycare that first day. Fears, guilt, and doubt weighed on me. I had taken all of that backup in Ohio for granted and now that the idea of getting "outside" help was no longer an abstract notion, I struggled emotionally.

As I mentioned, the bank that Greg and I worked for found positions for us before we moved. So by our second week, he and I both had to begin our new jobs. I was hired as a financial partner—meaning I would be in charge of a whole group of people. I remember vividly that first day of work. I was a shell of myself. There I was, trying to convince my team that I was a dependable, inspiring leader—that I had professional gravitas and gusto—when really it took everything I had to put a smile on my face and engage in small talk. But I told myself it was a new, exciting start.

Back to School Night at Faith's elementary school was held at the end of our second week. For us, it was the perfect chance to meet other families in the neighborhood. Conversely, it was also the first chance for people to get to know us. I wanted to give the best first impression, so I carefully assembled an outfit that, to me, said "put-together mom." It was neither too fancy nor too casual—a pair of short paper bag shorts from Target, a chambray top, and wedge heels. It was a look that exuded confidence without trying too hard; I felt it set the perfect tone.

That night, we pulled up in our SUV and, as I came to find out later, when I stepped down to get out of the car, my shorts hiked up, exposing my butt cheeks. And they stayed that way for the entire evening. I had no idea, but Greg did, and so did another mom who Greg witnessed giving me a dirty look of disapproval. Most partners probably would've either alerted their significant other or given the offending shorts a strong tug. No big deal. But given our history and the raw emotional state Greg was still in, he took it as a sign rather than an accident. His trust in me and my intentions was still so bruised and battered that it merely took the sight of the bottom of my ass to set him off. Seeing me somewhat exposed in the parking lot of our daughter's new school triggered a flood of insecurities and mistrust. In his mind, it was all happening once again, just as it had before. There I was, angling to get noticed by the neighborhood, by whatever means necessary. In that split second, his move to Florida switched from being a second chance for his family to being a new destination for him to be betrayed yet again. The weight of that pair of shorts and my exposed butt clobbered him with "evidence" that I hadn't changed. That's when I learned that triggers come in all forms, including body parts. And so, while we met some of the other parents and Faith's teacher, Greg was silently spiraling.

I had absolutely no idea.

When Back to School Night was over, we took the kids out to dinner. Greg and I ordered some beers and we had what I thought was a really nice evening. On the way home, Greg stopped to get a case of Coors Light and as soon as we got home began chugging can after can in the kitchen. I was with the kids, getting their pajamas on and settling in for a bedtime movie, having no idea what was brewing.

At some point in the evening, as the kids were dozing in our bed, Greg came in like a hurricane. Whipped up in a frenzy of pain, anger, heartbreak, and alcohol, he started pelting me with insults. That's when I learned about what happened with my outfit, but it didn't matter that it was the first time I'd heard about it. He had been stewing in his emotions and I could see the pain oozing out of his body. No amount of reasoning from me would have calmed him. In that moment, as I watched his frenzy, I realized how hard I had worked at convincing myself that Greg was over everything I'd done. I fooled myself into believing the worst was behind us because I desperately wanted the difficulty to be over. But that night I found myself literally being screamed at by the reality of my past betrayal.

The kids, who had been half-asleep, were woken up by a father they didn't recognize. I barely recognized him. He was so caught up in a story that he had created based off of his rage, his fears, our history, and my wardrobe malfunction that even when he was disparaging me, it was like he wasn't there.

I should be very clear here that at no point did I fear that I or the kids were in any physical danger. I was actually more concerned that Greg was going to accidentally hurt himself. True enough, he grabbed a framed wedding photo from the wall and cracked it over his knee with no regard for the glass that was broken by his brute force. He tackled our treadmill like he was in football practice, forcing a hole in the wall. He used his body as a weapon on himself and I didn't know how much it could take or when he would stop.

As worried as I was about Greg and his safety, my first concern was my kids. I had to get them out of there. Their dad was behaving in a way they had never seen before and they were scared. I couldn't imagine how things looked through their eyes, but I knew none of it was good. As quickly as I could, I grabbed one child in each arm and hustled outside and into the car. Greg's determination to shame me didn't abate. In his stupor, he followed us the whole way, spewing accusations and insults through his tightly clenched teeth. There we were, the newcomers on the block, wreaking havoc in this quiet suburban neighborhood. I ignored his offensive remarks and started the engine. To this day I don't know what our neighbors heard and thought that night. I knew someone might call the police. That there was a good chance Greg would call me from our neighborhood police station, wherever that was, needing to be picked up. But I had to go. If the police were called, I told myself that we would just figure it out then. While I felt responsible for being the original source of his pain and empathetic to his meltdown, it was his choice to drown himself in alcohol and make his tumult so unabashedly public. My heart was breaking at seeing the truth of how utterly shattered Greg was, but I told myself that the only thing I could control was ensuring my children were pulled out of the situation. So that's what I did. As I drove off that night, I could see Greg in my rearview mirror getting smaller and smaller. He watched us go, still held up by rage and beer.

Once I was in the car, I told the kids something along the lines of their daddy having too much to drink and feeling very upset. It was the best I could do and it was also the truth. Then I called good friends from Ohio. They were the only people we confided in about the affair. So while I talked to my girlfriend, her husband called Greg to help him calm down and make sure he was okay. If this had happened in Ohio, I would've had a long list of people I could turn to. But that night in Florida, I had nowhere to go. My friend advised me to check into a hotel. It was a good idea, but given our debt I wondered if my credit card would be declined. There were times we couldn't even fill up the gas tank. I had no idea whether I could afford a place to stay. And then what would I do? Where would I go? Would I just drive around all night? Would I find a parking lot and sleep in the car? There was literally no one who I could turn to for refuge and support. It was the loneliest I'd ever felt.

I decided to try a hotel. If we were turned away, then I would come up with some kind of plan B. As the kids and I walked into the hotel lobby late that night, I can only imagine the picture we made—me a mess from tears and despair, Faith in a pajama top and underwear, and Ben distraught and confused. We looked like a story you hear about "other people" (until you realize that you're only ever one alcohol-fueled night from becoming those "other people"). Sure enough, the desk manager asked me if I was okay in a tone and tenor that met the gravity of our appearance. I'll never forget the way he asked that question. I'm sure he was making a mental list of people he might have to call. The police, social services, etc. I told him everything was okay, and fortunately my credit card was accepted. I got the kids up to the room and right into bed, where they fell asleep quickly. Their bodies were too exhausted by the late hour and the stress to stay awake. With them asleep, I had nothing to do but process what had just transpired.

One stark difference between Greg and myself is that I don't tend to hold on to things. If something happens to me, I am typically able to process it pretty quickly and then release any associated feelings. Greg does not share that same quality. Even today, it can take him days to process things between us, when for me it might take a couple of hours. So I was unable to comprehend how raw he still was over everything. His feelings and the alcohol had driven him to the intersection of rage and adrenaline, causing catastrophic results.

My girlfriend told me that her husband had gotten Greg to calm down and that he was going to sleep it off. I got off of the phone and silently acknowledged this lowest of low points. I was humbled by the fierceness of Greg's feelings—feelings that both of us had so arrogantly assumed were under control. That whole quote about "wherever you go, there you are" was ringing in my ears. Florida had not solved our problems. It had just provided a new location for them to play out. That night my head was awash in scenarios of what my life might look like the next day. With no real answer as to which was the most likely, I fell asleep and waited for whatever reality rose with the sun.

The next morning I called Greg. I needed clothes for the kids. His voice was colored by shame and embarrassment. His sadness at behaving so abhorrently in front of them was palpable. He could no longer ignore the truth of what he was feeling about me, about our marriage, and about how wounded he was. And when he arrived at the hotel to bring us our stuff, his rage may have been drained, but the alcohol—it's noxious smell—was still swimming in his pores.

I checked out of the hotel and, while Greg slept off his hangover for most of the day, I took the kids out. I wanted there to be some distance between us until I knew that he and I could speak calmly and coherently.

At some point, when the kids weren't around, Greg and I finally talked. We agreed that neither one of us had any room left to fuck things up. We had each reached our allotment of turning our kids' lives upside down and both of us were committed to never putting them through anything like that again.

So what did that mean?

For Greg, the first thing it meant was that he would stop drinking. He knew that the only way he could guarantee that he would never put Faith and Ben through a similar experience was to commit to being sober. More than scaring us that night, I think Greg scared himself. I think he, too, had ignored how deeply hurt, vulnerable, and angry he still was at me. That it took only a single trigger, mixed with binge drinking, to catapult him into a combustible, uncontrollable situation, was a serious reality check for him. His behavior went against everything he believed in about what it meant to be a father, a husband, and a man.

When he told me he was going to quit drinking, I was relieved and supportive, though at that point, I was resistant to the idea that I needed to stop too. My ego happily reminded me that I was not the one who had lost control, so why would I need to choose sobriety as well? For both of us, drinking was never about a margarita or two. It was about a margarita *pitcher* or two. We had grown so accustomed to lubricating our experiences with alcohol that it had become the third "person" in our relationship. I have no doubt that our excessive drinking led both of us to the false impression that our relationship was more mended than it actually was. In actuality, I was busy mending while Greg was still processing everything. Back then, we had no consideration (or even awareness) of our different processing speeds. So while I was in the "moving forward" phase, he was still mired in a serious amount of doubt, sadness, and resentment—and when it became too much, he coped through drinking rather than working through it or speaking to anyone about it.

Greg didn't go to AA, but he had a close friend who went through NA, so he had someone that he could turn to for support and encouragement as he got used to this new lifestyle. And though I didn't stop drinking, his sobriety cut my drinking down by a lot. Our dates were stone-cold sober and Greg and I got to know each other in a completely new way (without the cocktail menu escape hatch). We *talked*, instead of partied. Removing the fuzz and blur of alcohol forced us to see each other as we were, all the time. And oddly enough, we liked each other more.

The second thing we both agreed needed to happen was a renewed commitment to work on our relationship. If we were going to build a solid marriage, we had to quit playing around and truly dig in and do it. Months of therapy wasn't enough. Moving wasn't enough. We needed to work harder. We jointly made the decision that day to stop trying to get over things and start trying to get through them.

Greg and I began reading books on infidelity and discussing them as they related to our experience and feelings. We started actively applying some of the tools we'd learned in therapy too. This work unleashed our curiosity on how to become better individuals, knowing that it would inevitably lead to a better, healthier marriage. We continually recommitted to doing this work even as bumps emerged.

I've always loved and admired Greg, but the work and effort we put in at that time opened the door to me really *liking* him. Although by that point we'd been together for nearly a decade, this was the first time he and I both started to feel truly seen and heard.

Believe me, I know that this story could have had many endings, and I am not advocating for the choices that Greg and I made. Us choosing to recommit to each other that next day, rather than dissolve our marriage, was based on what we knew about each other and who we were as people. And let me say that if you ever feel in danger or physically or emotionally abused by your significant other, I strongly encourage you to find your way out of that relationship. No amount of relationship work can take the place of feeling emotionally and physically safe. For Greg, that night was a wake-up call—both in regard to his reliance on drinking as well as the reality of where he truly stood with me and our marriage. I think I can safely say that if Greg had not made the choice that next day to stop drinking or if he and I had not mutually decided to work our asses off to understand each other better and respect one another's feelings more, then the outcome might have turned out very differently. But we did do those things. And I believe that's why I can happily say that no such night like the one I just shared has ever occurred again. Not even close. But let's be clear. That was not because of dumb luck. It was not because of faith in one another. And it certainly wasn't because of some romantic notion of sticking together through hard times. It was because we were determined to work furiously on what our marriage meant to us, on understanding who we were as individuals, and then allowing that to inform what we wanted and needed out of our relationship.

And so we began the climb out of our mutual, rockiest bottom.

RESETTING YOUR MARRIAGE OR PARTNERSHIP

Miscommunication

These days, there is almost nothing that I wouldn't share with Greg. There's almost nothing we can't talk about. We, of course, still have disagreements and we still even argue, but it's completely different than it once was. When one of us is having a visceral reaction to something or if we're triggered from a past trauma, we're more likely to address it curiously—to dig into and explore it. On our best days, we're like feelings detectives who try to discover the what, when, and why of what we're experiencing. Back then, however, negative or complicated feelings were either stifled and pushed down or expressed as weapons of an "I'm right, you're wrong" war. There was no learning or understanding; there was only winning.

Until we went into therapy, until my affair was discovered, and until we had that devastating argument in Florida, Greg and I hadn't fully figured out how to actually talk to one another. It seems crazy that you can be with someone for years, raise children with them, consider them to be your best friend, and realize that all that time you weren't truly *talking* to each other. I know he and I aren't alone in this discovery, that scores of other people have also realized how little they shared with their partner, but it seems wild when you really sit down and think about it. I should also mention that, for Greg and me, when we began our relationship, it was after years of feeling like the universe was determined to put us together. It was like we were unknowingly in our own little Reese Witherspoon romantic comedy. So if you feel like destiny has weighed in on your romance, why would you ever think that something as common and mundane as communication would get in your way?

Our kids love to hear the prequel to our relationship—all of the run-intos and unofficial dates. They think it's cool that their dad and I saw the band Leo together on an is-this-a-date-or-not outing because over time, Leo would figure prominently in our romance, so much so that it's Ben's middle name. Faith loves that the first time I saw Greg at an after-party, I thought to myself, *I'm going to marry that guy*. Seeing as I was still with Bob at the time and that Greg and I only chitchatted, the thought was ridiculous. But it was there—like a thought bubble that quickly disperses into a puff of smoke. My kids also can't believe I hired Greg's band to play at my prom. How Greg's younger brother—their uncle—even tried to get Greg to go to the after-party. He refused because he was five years older and had no interest in high school parties. Faith and Ben think it's amazing that we were in each other's presence without realizing how intertwined our futures would become. They also think it's crazy how, for the next two years, life would continue to put us in front of one another until we finally got the message and began dating.

Greg and I love our lead-up story too—how can we not when the universe put us together even when we were 500 miles from home in Manhattan—one of the most populated cities in the country? It's amazing when you think about it. That trip was so significant to both of us that Manhattan is Faith's middle name.

We couldn't ignore all of the signs, happenstances, and coincidences that kept throwing us together.

Once we were in a relationship, Greg and I understood that neither of us would be beholden to the rules of the "shoulds." As I said earlier, he and I were dreamers, and we were proud of it. So our early time together was more about taking the world by storm than it was about working through our different communication styles. And, let's be honest, when you're in the honeymoon phase of a relationship, it's not very sexy to talk about your communication baggage.

I also have to admit that our shared interest in partying probably contributed to our lack of transparency when it came to expressing our feelings. We were of the mind that blowing off steam and getting drunk, taking a Vicodin or some other good-time pill, would solve our problems for us—even if "solving" meant forgetting. After all, it was fun, and fun was good for any relationship, right? Alcohol, drugs, late nights—they were the perfect accompaniment to the hours we spent working our asses off professionally. It was the old work hard, play hard mentality. For us, this lifestyle was a commonality. It was one of the reasons we both felt like we were made for each other. For us, it just worked. At least that's what we thought at the time.

We worked. We played. We partied. We got pregnant.

Maybe had we waited a bit longer to start a family, we would've had more of an opportunity to figure out healthier conflict resolution habits. Maybe. It's true that we had almost no time to work through (or even discover) communication pitfalls that we'd spend years falling into. But in all honesty, I don't think either of us realized how problematic the ways in which we chose to express ourselves were. And you can't fix what you don't even understand is a problem.

At warp speed our union went from fun and games to

we-better-not-f-this-up. It was a bumpy transition. For my part, I was a mere twenty-two years old, just beginning to feel my independence and some financial freedom. Greg, who is five years older, had more life experience, but he was focused on pouring most of his energy into his newly found passion for finance and sales. And neither of us had any experience in sharing a household with a significant other. It was definitely dizzying. But I should be clear that neither of us were unhappy nor burdened by the pregnancy news. Though outside of the typical order of things, Greg and I both understood that we were "it" for each other, so having the baby made sense to us—even if it was eyebrow raising for others. In truth, I was once in a similar situation. But in that case, I was absolutely sure that it wasn't the right time, and so I made the choice to have an abortion. This pregnancy, for so many reasons, felt completely different: I had a career, I was with the person I wanted to spend my life with, and I could so much more easily envision the pathway to parenthood before me. So although the two situations weren't too terribly far apart from one another chronologically, they were miles from one another when it came to the circumstances. So there we were, anxious and excited to play house.

As many of you already know, nothing shines a brighter light on all of the cracks that exist in your relationship like parenthood. Greg and I hadn't yet worked out the vastly different family cultures that we grew up in. We hadn't had long romantic conversations about the types of parents we wanted to be. We hadn't really thought about how much being in charge of another human reduces the time available for dreaming about that "big" life. All of those cracks would've been fine; no couple can anticipate every bump in the road that emerges once you have children. However, if your communication rituals are more about winning than resolving, those issues go from cracks to chips to all-out broken pieces.

I call them "communication rituals" because when I think back on them now, that's what they reminded me of. A ritual. We all have them. It's how we know what buttons to push or not to push in order to lead a disagreement in one direction or the other. It's the reason we know when something has escalated. And it's the way we know that if we make one more comment, a tense discussion will blow up into a full-on argument. For Greg and me, our ritual went something like this:

- I begin the silent treatment but do everything with major attitude.
- Greg pushes me to tell him what's wrong.
- I finally give in and yell at him about the problem.
- He clams up when I raise my voice, which only makes me angrier.
- I explode.
- We find ourselves in separate rooms after first insult-bombing each other.
- We don't discuss it again.

And nothing gets truly resolved.

Greg and I followed this ritual not because it was satisfying. We did it because we just didn't know any better. In order to communicate effectively, you have to first be able to understand what it is that you're really feeling. And if you're lucky (or exceptionally self-aware), you're also able to decipher why. Unfortunately neither of us gave ourselves the space to explore the what and the why of our emotions.

Anger, jealousy, anxiety, and other such negative emotions aren't experienced in a vacuum. It's rare for those feelings to emerge as a pure iteration of that single emotion. And so, for me, what I was feeling and how it presented itself were sometimes two entirely different things. As you well know, anger and rage were my go-to emotions—no matter what was actually rumbling underneath. And more often than not, especially in the first couple of years of our relationship, what I was really feeling was insecurity and fear of abandonment. It just happened to come out as bitchy, bitter anger.

All of my life I worked really hard to appear bulletproof. Underneath, though, I was actually pretty insecure. Competition and the spotlight were ways for me to distract everyone from the mush of self-doubt I felt. If I could prove my worth to others through winning, being the life of the party, or getting straight A's, then nobody would be able to see that sensitive vulnerability that lay just below the surface. Coupled with my insecurity was a latent fear of abandonment. As you know, my parents raised me to be independent, often leaving me alone if they had to work or wanted to go out somewhere or run an errand. This started from about the age of six. And while I loved it most of the time, there were some days I just didn't want to be left alone. I can recall once throwing a ceramic dish at the front door moments after my parents went out somewhere. But I made sure I only acted out like this when I was alone and no one could witness my vulnerability. In my mind, it would only show weakness, and that was simply unacceptable.

Early on in our relationship, Greg and I were flying high on love and possibility. I wanted him to see me as this pillar of strength who took the world by storm. Hell, I wanted to see myself that way too. In my mind, showing a softer side had no place in that image. So the only time I ever addressed any of the aspects of our relationship that gave me pause was through anger. For example, I didn't want to show Greg that his "rock star" past sometimes made me unsure of his fidelity (even though he never gave me a reason to doubt him). I couldn't explain how betrayed I felt when we hung out with his family and Greg would take their side over mine. And when he made plans with his band or his buddies to play video games or spend the weekend away, I certainly didn't want to share that this made me feel as if my company wasn't enough for him.

Instead of revealing all of those complex feelings, I held on to them. I filed those perceived slights away so I could cherry-pick them whenever they'd have the greatest impact. I'd add up all of Greg's wrongs and lob them at him like a grenade. Greg would go on the defensive by name-calling. He'd wield the "crazy" moniker around like a sword. A hole would get punched into the wall. Or water would be thrown. Queso even ended up on our ceiling in one epic battle. Our arguments typically ended because shit needed to be cleaned up, not because we resolved anything. We'd exhaust ourselves into a detente—until the next time.

I know what you're thinking… if queso is going to end up shellacked to the ceiling or water is going to be thrown into someone's face, then surely it was for a good reason. You might assume the causes of these arguments were significant. But you'd be wrong. Amazingly, it was more common for tensions to ignite over small slights than anything big. For example, when Greg had the opportunity to tour for six weeks with the band Leo—that same band he and I saw on our unofficial first date—it didn't matter to me that Faith was a toddler. I wanted him to take advantage of the opportunity. I told him to go. Even though he was leaving us for an extended period of time, I still felt like I was part of it. Greg could never have left his family like that without the support of his partner, so even though I wasn't there physically, I was definitely there in spirit. And yet, when Greg would go off with his friends at the last minute or tell me he was spending a night away to hang out with the band, I would just about lose my mind, my anger building to the point of queso suddenly taking flight.

I can remember one particular weekend that Greg spent out of town with his bandmates. I was told it was a guys' weekend—no wives or girlfriends. However, when he and I spoke the next morning, I could hear female voices in the background. This sent me into a tailspin. As it turned out, some of the wives decided to join them at the last minute, no big deal. But what I felt was utter rejection and betrayal. I berated him on the phone, not giving a shit that he was sitting at a table with his friends and their wives. Greg's embarrassment at my accusations and how I dealt with my feelings only extended the argument further to when he got home. I knew I'd blown up, but I couldn't stop myself. I didn't know how.

I didn't know how to explain to him that infidelity was common in my world. I couldn't hold his promiscuous past against him when my own wasn't exactly saintly. I had little faith in any kind of foundation of trust even though Greg had never even hinted at fooling around. It was embedded in my mind because that was what I was most familiar with. People cheat. So instead of talking to him about any of it, I raged and blamed.

Greg too had issues that he didn't know how to talk about. In fact, there were some things he kept hidden for years. It was only during our time in therapy that I discovered that Greg's drug use was more extensive than my own. Once I was pregnant, I thought we decided to stop taking any pills. This was before the opioid epidemic was in full effect, but we mutually decided to stop using drugs when we partied. We still drank to our heart's content, but I was under the impression that that was it. You can imagine my surprise when I learned years later that Greg had continued. Pills, pot, whatever it was... Greg would partake in it behind my back. He just couldn't find his way to telling me.

He also struggled to navigate conflict with his family. As I mentioned previously, he played out his jester role while I wondered where the Greg I lived with went. I've always loved his sense of humor, but it morphed into this sophomoric silliness when he was around his family. I would watch as he bent himself around their expectations of who they thought he was. But outside of fighting about it, we never really discussed why he acted that way.

When it came to our families, we unfortunately slid easily into the "my family does [insert chosen subject here], while your family doesn't ..." Comparing our families and the culture we grew up in was rife with land mines. It was like resentment fertilizer that grew weeds of animosity. The one thing we could agree on was how lucky we were that Greg's parents, who were retired, basically made themselves available all the time for us. We were both incredibly grateful for it. My parents, on the other hand, were only available every so often on weekends, because they lived further away and were still working full-time. And while I understood how generous Greg's parents were for giving us so much of their time, my gratitude didn't stamp out my need for space and boundaries. Greg always took my desire for separation and privacy as being ungrateful for their help. He couldn't understand how I could complain about things since his family had stepped up so much while mine was only available sporadically. He also grew up in an environment where everyone was very involved in each other's lives, so it didn't bother him like it did me. Independence was highly valued in my household. Our different perspectives unsurprisingly drew subtle battle lines. And, over time, the more we relied on his parents' help, the more our tensions grew and the more exaggerated our problems became.

Peacefully co-charting this rocky territory of gratitude, obligation, boundaries, and pure family time seemed impossible. So instead of talking, we became more distant and filed away more hurts. Extended family became one more thing we couldn't talk about honestly.

Greg and I slowly disappeared from each other's view. We still lived our life. We still even enjoyed each other. But we weren't truly seeing one another.

Cracks. Chips. Broken pieces. We spent years sweeping them up into a pile of communication fails. It was only after we sought out therapy that we had to take all of those broken shards and piece them back together to create a new mosaic of understanding. That brought us steps closer to learning how to truly talk to one another, which transformed our relationship. And yet, there was another piece that we still had to figure out. And that was intimacy. It had virtually vanished, and we would never find our way back to one another without it.

RESETTING YOUR MARRIAGE OR PARTNERSHIP

The Intimacy Personality Test

"*Your emotional love language and the language of your spouse may be as different as Chinese from English...*" This quote, from *The 5 Love Languages* by Dr. Gary Chapman, felt like it was written specifically for Greg and me. Along with our different communication styles, Greg and I gave and received love in totally divergent ways, but we had no idea back then, and it would be a long journey of figuring it out.

Let me get this out of the way first: Sex itself was never a problem for us. Greg and I have always been attracted to one another. We've always satisfied each other sexually as well. Thankfully, our issues didn't ever have to do with what was happening under the sheets, so to speak. Though that also meant that our intimacy issues weren't obvious. We couldn't point to anything tangible and both agree that that was it! Instead, our issues were due to a miasma of things—daily life, past experiences, and just generally different ways of looking at sex, intimacy, and how we expressed our love for one another.

When Greg and I first started dating, sex—prioritizing it and doing it—was easy. Showing affection was second nature. Our lives were about our careers, having a good time, and being together. Intimacy and expressing our love weren't issues because we had so much time and space—both physically and emotionally—to keep that at the top of our priority list. We also desired one another greatly. Like most couples early on in their relationship, Greg and I were bewitched by the potency of newness. We never shied away from PDA and could always be found snuggling. Our friends would laugh and roll their eyes at our inability to keep our hands off of one another. So when I was told by one of them to "just wait," to see how things would slow down, I didn't quite believe her.

I'll also admit that another reason why our sex life was so good was because I was determined to make it so. At that point in my life, sex and my self-worth were tightly woven together. I had always looked for outside confirmation that I was attractive and sexy and had no inkling that those feelings could be sustained from within. I sought out that validation—but not too aggressively, because I didn't want to be deemed a slut either! I needed to be just desirable enough so I could sustain my self-worth while maintaining my "good girl" halo. So satisfying Greg's desires was, in part, a way for me to feel good about myself. To feel worthy of him. Without Greg even realizing it, he played a starring role in my complex understanding of intimacy, sex, and self-confidence.

Deepening my insecurity was my own amazement that I'd finally landed *that* guy—the one that my gut told me I was going to marry. The one I kept running into. The rock star. Greg was the person I felt fated to be with. But once I had him, I was anxious about my ability to hold on to him. What if I wasn't enough? How could I hold a candle to the images I'd conjured up of the women he'd been with previously? Groupies. Women who look like they should be in music videos. Surely Greg's sexual resume included people who knew way more about sex than I did. Undoubtedly they were more fun in bed too. There was no comparison between me and the women I cast in my mind as Greg's past partners. But rather than explore that self-doubt with him, I treated the symptom. I consented to sex whenever he wanted. Thankfully, our drive was pretty similar before Faith was born. However, on the occasional night I wasn't in the mood or felt tired from the day, I refused to allow myself to share it with him. Just as I wanted him to think of me as bulletproof, I also wanted him to think of me as someone who always shared his enthusiasm and confidence about having sex. I believed exposing my vulnerabilities was unattractive and a surefire knockout punch to my desirability.

Being the PDA superstars that we were, Greg and I not only had exclusive access to one another's personal space, we also made it a practice to surprise each other with sweet notes of affection—a balloon, a thoughtful card—some romantic token to let the other know that we were thinking of them. For Greg, all of these small acts naturally segued into the bigger finale of sex. If not in that very moment, then sometime in the not too distant future. I wouldn't go so far as to say that it's the reason why he went out of his way to do those sweet things though. Greg, by nature, is very romantic. However, for him it was all part of a larger goal—to have and maintain intimate relations with each other. For me, those sweet treats were stand-alone moments—shot glass portions that connected us to one another. Even before we had kids, I didn't always need the finale. And in my mind, intimacy, acts of love, also extended to our home. Cooking dinner. Cleaning the house. That was another way I showed Greg that I cared for him.

Our wedding night is a great example of our different ideas about expressing love. Faith was two when Greg and I decided to marry. We paid for the event ourselves, so we kept the guest list to our closest friends and family. After the ceremony and dinner, we moved on to a local venue where we'd hired a band to play. It was more frat party than wedding reception though, and Greg and I spent most of the night milling about with other people. After that, there was the after-party, which was fittingly at my hometown's neighborhood bar—the one where my dad had first heard Greg's band play, the one where we shared a stolen kiss while I was still in college. We drank and partied some more; the familiar bar crowd celebrating our nuptials right alongside us. Greg even hopped up onstage and took over the drums at one point. It was a blast.

After closing down that bar, he and I hopped into our limo with Greg's brother and his wife. They were headed home and we were headed to our hotel for our first night as husband and wife. Within the first few minutes of the drive, I threw up. I had aimed for the Styrofoam cooler we'd packed into the limo, but I missed and vomited all over my sparkly wedding dress instead. Seconds later I passed out on Greg's lap. Greg only lasted a few moments more and ended up passing out while leaning over me, his Coors Light resting on my hip. My brother-in-law captured the moment with his camera, so we can forever remember our wild wedding. Forty minutes later we were dropping my brother and sister-in-law at their house. Then we stopped off at a gas station to grab some supplies: chocolate milk, Marlboro Lights, and donuts. I can't recall how I managed to enter the hotel but I do have a vague memory of lying on the floor of the lobby, shoeless, and still wearing my vomit-covered wedding dress. Greg guided me to our room and I immediately passed out on the bed. He sat in the chair for a while in the dark, smoking and drinking the chocolate milk. And that was our wedding night.

The next day, as we drove to our honeymoon cabin in the hills, Greg revealed how hurt and disappointed he was that we hadn't consummated our marriage on our first official night as husband and wife. I was surprised. Hadn't we had an amazing wedding? Outside of ruining my dress, hadn't it been a night to remember? We had the time of our lives, didn't we? And it wasn't as if we'd never had sex before—we had a child together already! Was having sex on that "first" night that important? Yes. To him it was.

Though future conversations didn't carry the weight of a wedding night, the tension over when, how often, and how important sex was would follow us for years.

With children comes gravity. Greg and I could no longer float on love and possibility. We were permanently grounded. "Adulting" had a completely different definition now. Before the weight of a little human's life is put on you, bad decisions and mistakes—missing bill payments, career changes, too many late nights, not taking care of yourself—aren't that big of a deal. But take on the responsibility of another person and suddenly poor choices take on much greater significance. It can be exhausting. This is not to say that Greg and I don't enjoy being parents. We absolutely do. Being a mom is, by far, my favorite role. It's just that once kids were in the picture, every decision felt more important. I was needed in a new way. So was Greg. And need meant demands—on me, on him—and so the demands on "we," as a couple, started getting ignored.

If we were each other's top priority pre-kids, then post-kids we were lucky if we made it to second on the list. On crazier days our relationship would *maybe* make it into the top five. The rigors and responsibilities of parenthood always felt more important than anything else. Conversations between us were often limited to the happenings in our household. Here's my to-do list, here's yours. Faith has this after-school activity, Ben has that...

And none of it was sexy.

With little quality time at home, we did what every relationship expert tells you to do—we had date nights! We went out. We got wasted. Together. We partied with our friends and stayed out late. We nursed hangovers. Together. Back then we both believed that was how we bonded. That's how we connected—that's how we always connected. Going out for us always meant getting away from responsibility. Blowing off steam. It never occurred to us that as our life got more complicated that we might need to set aside specific time to connect more deeply with one another. And when the stress of my daily task list began to plague me with anxiety, it created tension between Greg and me in ways that we hadn't felt before. And the thicker the tension got, the less we thoughtfully communicated about it. Actually, if we didn't yell about it, we didn't discuss it at all. Without realizing it, we were pulling away from each other and, unsurprisingly, drunken date nights didn't help to bring us back together. If anything, they helped us stay disconnected.

Once I was back at work, I would spend my days bending over backwards to meet the demands of clients. Cameo the Career Woman was in full effect. Then I'd come home and go right into Cameo the Supermom: homework, dinner, cleaning, bath, story time, etc. Once that was done, I'd crash between nine and ten so that I could get up and do it all again the next day. Greg has always been a night owl. He'd often start work back up again or go do something he enjoyed after he and I put the kids to bed. He liked eking out more hours from the day. I couldn't function this way, and so, even when we were together in the same physical space, we weren't really with each other. When Greg did finally come to bed, there was usually at least one of the kids there too, putting a literal wedge between us. The co-sleeping began as a way for me to get as much sleep as possible while I was breast-feeding. Then it just continued because I loved the sentimentality and comfort of it. Greg didn't enjoy it as much as I did, but he acquiesced more to keep the peace than anything else. Besides, even when we did put the kids in their own beds at nighttime, we usually fell asleep with them. So no matter what we did, our nights often found us separated somehow.

Over time, our sex life was really diminished. All of the PDA had mostly disappeared too. We were still cuddling—but it was usually with one of our kids instead of with each other. I can remember feeling annoyed when Greg would come up behind me to give me a playful hug while I was doing the dishes. I was too focused on getting shit done to feel wooed in anyway. I wouldn't say we had gotten to the point of being roommates, but I definitely understood what my friend meant when she warned me that our sex life would slow down as time went on. And Greg really missed it. It's not that I didn't; it's just that I had so many other things on my mind. I was much more easily distracted by everything happening in the day-to-day. How could I get in the mood when I knew I had to get up early to make sure the kids were ready for school? How could I find the time when the floors needed to be cleaned? How could I concentrate on making love when I had that big meeting the next day? And even when I did feel the slightest bit randy, I was usually also so damn tired. Greg, on the other hand, was perpetually ready. His ability to switch his sex drive on like a light switch boggled my mind. For me, getting in the mood was more akin to an engine that didn't want to start on a cold morning. It took time and warmth. Neither felt readily available to me.

The lack of intimacy in our relationship when the kids were young carried a different kind of weight for me than it did for Greg. For him, our lack of time together meant that he must not be that important to me, which I couldn't understand. Hadn't he noticed how clean the floors were? Didn't he enjoy the home-cooked meal I'd made? Or that he never ran out of clean shirts for work? Couldn't he see that I was doing those things for him, for us? No, it felt as if all he paid attention to was our lack of a sex life. One night when I was too tired to be anything but brutally honest, I basically said, "I give myself to everyone else all day. I don't have anything left for you." It was the truth, and it was soul crushing for him. My mind and my body were being pulled at all day long, so adding one more thing that would require more of me both physically and mentally was just too much. Part of me resented him for asking more of me than I could give. I wanted to *want* to have sex. I wanted Greg to feel important and desired. But I simply didn't have it in me. Understandably, Greg didn't see anything the way I did. He couldn't separate my feelings about having sex with how I felt about him. I would learn much later after reading Chapman's book that it was because his love language was so different from my own. Back then, however, without that understanding, we both just felt hurt and frustrated with each other.

As our ability to communicate with one another deteriorated, so too did our sense of intimacy. We were a family, yes, but we were barely participants in our marriage. Sex typically only happened when we were intoxicated. And though I would've said at the time that Greg was my best friend and my go-to party buddy, my belief that it was us against the world had faded.

My rebellions came along soon after. As did my deep dive into athletic endeavors, pulling my focus even further away from Greg and any sense of empathy I'd had about his feelings. I was tangled up with lies and guilt but sold it as irritation. Greg bristled with resentment and loneliness. Feeling ignored and unheard, he was also unwilling to consider my perspective on things. In our own way, we were both on edge and tense, which are two of the least sexy emotions a couple can feel. Then, while out on a date night, couple friends of ours sang the praises of Chapman's book. Greg and I ordered two copies right there and then. It opened up a whole new world of understanding. It broadened the idea of intimacy for us so that it was no longer this oversimplified understanding of what a sex life includes. We began to view it as an unspoken language that's communicated through copious actions throughout the day.

Clearly, sex was very important to Greg, but I didn't fully comprehend why. He'd lived the rock star lifestyle for a while, so I assumed sex for him was simply about how much and with whom. I took my knowledge of his past promiscuity to mean that he loved it because of the pleasure it gave him. It took time for me to understand that pleasure was only part of it. For him, sex was about sharing an experience and enjoying each other. When I presumed it was just about him having a good time, it felt like another task I was being asked to do, but once I understood that it was truly his way of connecting with me, it felt more like something for us, rather than something I needed to do for him. One seemed like an errand, the other like a sweet escape. And that made a big difference in my mind.

I also had to untangle my own confusing feelings around sex. Truth bomb: I had quite the promiscuous past. Frankly, sex was attached to my self-worth and I had to learn how to separate the two. The process of doing this forced me to confront feelings of shame and negativity around my sexuality. Like so many women, I was subliminally taught that enjoying sex meant that I was somehow a "bad girl." That having multiple partners outside of relationships or one-night stands was not something a woman did. If she did behave that way, then she'd definitely need to hide it. I hadn't realized just how powerful those messages had been. As it turned out, they'd played a big influence on my life—even in my marriage. I made assumptions and projected my own feelings around having sex onto Greg. One epiphany for me was realizing that sex, for me, didn't lead to connection. I liked it, but it was more about getting acceptance, feeling worthy, or being drunk. Boom. That was a huge realization. This work with Greg gave me the opportunity to redefine what being intimate with him meant to me.

Once we comprehended that neither of us were right or wrong but rather just speaking different "languages," we could turn our focus from blame to understanding. While I worked to make sense of Greg's beliefs around intimacy, he had to do the same with mine. We had to learn to respect and "speak" in the other's love language. This took work and a lot of practice, which is ongoing. But similar to the way we had to learn how to communicate with one another, learning how to express intimacy required us both to be vulnerable. Basically, Greg and I had to check our egos at the door and push the Reset Button on just about every aspect of our relationship.

RESETTING YOUR MARRIAGE OR PARTNERSHIP

Hitting the Reset Button on Your Relationship

It was just two weeks after our big move to Florida that Greg and I had that explosive argument and I found myself in a hotel room, emotionally depleted, distraught, and feeling very alone. Clearly we hadn't gotten past, gotten over, or pushed through everything the way we'd convinced ourselves we had. It was a bleak and dark low point. But from conversations during the immediate aftermath, a few things did become illuminated. The first was that we were both indisputably committed to our family and our marriage. The second was that he and I were still in undeniable pain. And the third was that this rockiest of bottoms was going to be the foundation for a new marriage. We wanted to tear down who and what we once were to each other and rebuild from where we were at this honest, though ugly, point.

Though Greg and I knew we were both committed to making our relationship work, neither of us were sure how to proceed. In fact, to be totally honest with you, after the explosion, I made things even worse by reaching out to *him* one last time. I was like an addict going back for the high. Once again, Greg discovered my text and confronted me about it. It only made him trust me less (which I didn't think was possible), but amazingly he didn't want to give up. Neither did I. You can imagine then how low our starting point was when we began this work. It was like starting from zero. No, below zero, which, by the way, isn't synonymous with a clean slate. It was anything but. There was still pain and so much tainted history that we had to come to terms with. With little direction and few concrete ideas, we decided to start backwards. Our work began by discussing what we wanted our marriage to look like on the other side of this process. From there, we figured we could backtrack.

We both had ideas and relationship goals for the Future Cameo and Greg. We wanted to have a mutual sense of safety, as well as the space, respect, and empathy to communicate honestly with one another. We wanted to feel supported, not just inside of our marriage and family but also with our outside endeavors. He and I also talked about the desire to feel valued and appreciated through a strong emotional and physical connection. And finally, we were determined to remain a cohesive unit. Neither of us wanted to break up our family, which meant that no matter how hard the work got, no matter how vulnerable we needed to be, we needed to keep at it.

Keeping our goals at the forefront of our minds, we dug in and got started. There was no relationship GPS, no Siri for marriages, so we decided to let our instincts be our guide. We engaged in the activities that helped us previously, like reading and just simply talking to one another. We did our best to validate the other's feeling, but inevitably there are always bumps, detours, and treacherous curves. So when shit went down, like disagreements and flat-out arguments, we did our best (meaning, sometimes we failed with a capital F) not to repeat old habits. No more name-calling. No more comparisons. No more throwing the past in the other's face. Sometimes, we'd just have to walk away from one another and cool down first. Other times one of us was the MVP of couple goals, while the other failed miserably. But we just kept trying.

I know I'm painting quite the rosy picture, but trust me when I tell you that there were times where it was anything but. I'm not going to lie; there were points while doing this work when we wondered if a truly good marriage was a myth the likes of Atlantis and unicorns. We both realized how freaking hard it is to set judgment aside. It's equally hard to ask for what you need. And it's even harder to do all of that while in the midst of everyday life.

Listening to Greg without judgment at first felt like there was a boxing match in my brain between this new way of being and my good ol' ego. As Greg shared his needs with me, the internal fight began between the partner I was striving to be and the ego I'd grown so used to listening to. My thoughts had to bob and weave away from my ego's instincts. It was rough for a while, but thankfully the more I practiced not ceding control, the more my ego was knocked out for the count. Greg had a similar experience as well. So those small victories, along with our shared commitment to stay together, is what kept us trudging forward.

As lucky as I was that we had both committed to putting in the work, I was also aware of the possibility that we could grow in different directions. There were days that anxiety plagued me as my mind ran off with all of the possible "what-ifs." What if he doesn't like who I am or who I become? What if we don't see things the same way anymore? What if I don't like him? What if he wasn't comfortable being so far away from Ohio? What if he never trusts me again? What if we were only held together by our love for partying and drinking? Or worse, what if we didn't like ourselves or who we were together?

As I had discovered after the work I did on myself, the only way to quell "what-if" syndrome was to bring myself back to the present through stillness. I had to remind myself that *today* we were still together. *Today* was all we had. The ugly truth was also that one or a number of these "what-if's" could have come to fruition. I had to accept and make peace with that. I also reminded myself that mutually working toward the goal of becoming better versions of ourselves would naturally translate into becoming better partners.

Our second understanding—that we were both still suffering from an enormous amount of pain—was especially challenging for me. Slowly, through my individual work, I realized I'd spent the better part of my life pushing past pain, both physical and emotional. Even admitting that I was struggling was hard for me. I took pride in being fine, in pulling off being pulled-together. Even validating Greg's pain came with challenges. I often found myself hurrying him along with his feelings or dismissing the validity of his pain as a way to push through. Without really admitting it, I had convinced myself that when we moved, we left our rawest, ugliest parts behind. Ohio was where our pain was. Florida was where our fresh-start future would be. But the truth was that our emotional gas tank was running on fumes. It had gotten us to our destination, but we'd now have to trek on foot if we wanted to build an authentically healed and happy life. And in order to do that, I'd have to find a way to be okay with sitting in my own (and Greg's) darkest feelings.

Greg and I took our third understanding—that we would rebuild our marriage—very seriously. In fact, we often look at it as if we've been married twice. We had our old marriage, which ended with me and the kids in a hotel room and him angrily weeping in our house. That gave way to our second union, which came along just a few days later. Our first was mired in a result-oriented mindset. We were all about the destination instead of the good and bad of whatever had gotten us there. For example, when my affair was first revealed, he and I so badly wanted things between us to be better, so instead of truly being honest about how we were feeling, we focused more on doing and saying all the "right" things. Performative healing, rather than the truer, messier kind. It didn't matter that we did it for all good, mushy reasons. We loved each other. We wanted to be "us" again—the us we remembered from our early days together. But that "us" now had two children, more experience, and a hell of a lot more baggage. And, if I'm honest, that "us" was buried under layers of labels, assumptions, and expectations. Back then I built a lot of my relationship with Greg on the things I wanted him to see, rather than on showing him my authentic self. I hid my insecurities and vulnerabilities. I hid myself. Rebuilding our marriage based on how we remembered who we once were would've been like building something from sand. The only sturdy foundation was the one that included the resentment, the heartbreak, the sadness, and, yes, the vulnerabilities. Being truly transparent about how we were actually feeling about our partnership was the only concrete solution to creating the durable relationship we were striving for.

Our first step in our process was to assess our priorities. Greg and I essentially established a metaphorical relationship jar to help us stay focused on the important parts of our union. Similar to the way my personal priorities had been determined by meaningfulness, our marriage priorities were determined by understanding the nonnegotiable needs we had for each other. That started with the most basic and seemingly obvious qualities of a relationship: communication, commitment, and intimacy. But the not so obvious aspect was how these nonnegotiables meant something different for Greg than they did for me, so we also needed to translate that difference for one another.

Clear communication is essential in a healthy relationship, but it's especially so when trust has been broken and your teamwork has been thrown out the window. When Greg and I looked back at how we related to each other, we realized just how false our sense of "us" was. In truth, it was more like "me versus you." If he got to go out with his buddies, I'd make him pay by being nasty and disgruntled, so he'd think twice before he went out again. If he picked up the slack while I trained for a competition, he'd slather on the guilt and hint at my selfishness, so I would remember the next time I committed to a new fitness goal. It was a kind of dirty, immature scorekeeping.

We also dove into our individual needs, which can be scary as hell. Not only was it tough to admit what we needed for ourselves, it was also sometimes head-bangingly hard to accept what the other person needs in exchange. My return to the fitness world is a great example. As much as Greg understood that my intentions for getting back into that world were pure, and as much as he wanted to support this need, it also set off alarm bells inside of him. Getting back into a gym meant, for him, stepping right back into the same period of time when I was unfaithful. He feared me sliding right back into old habits. In our previous marriage, Greg would've kept his feelings quiet. The resentment and anxiety building right on top of those old, raw hurts. But beyond passive-aggressive comments, he wouldn't have shared any of it. As for me, I would've pushed and bullied, essentially telling him to get over it until I "won." I would've resented his feelings and his need to hold me back. In short, it would've been an epic battle of wills in which more queso or whatever food was around at the moment would've gotten stuck to the ceiling.

In our new marriage, Greg shared his fears with me. In all honesty, I found his concerns frustrating, but that didn't mean they weren't valid. He understood my need to work out, so he also wasn't suggesting I stop. Where once we would have angrily retreated to our corners, we worked on navigating a solution in which we both felt comfortable and heard. Instead of going to battle we worked it out together.

Greg and I realized through this work that we would have to cozy up to the idea that things were sometimes going to get emotional, uncomfortable, and ugly. The process of creating a formidable union is pretty messy. But as long as patience and empathy are superglued to all of that mess, you can make it to the other side. We also informally created some expectations and ground rules related to this work. Things like accepting and respecting the other's thoughts and feelings. Mutually agreeing on boundaries and the expectation that our feelings be met with compassion. And just because one of us felt triggered by something, it didn't make it true, nor did it make it the other's fault. And lastly, we agreed that, above all, we would be honest with each other. They say "honesty is the best policy," but I would bet that no one has ever said "honesty is the *easiest* policy."

As we grew more comfortable and confident in ourselves and our ability to navigate our own feelings, we communicated them more effectively to each other. From there, we relied once again on books.

Cue *The 5 Love Languages*.

As I mentioned before, we both read this insightful book. Once finished, we completed the Love Languages assessment. Of the five categories used in the book, we discovered that mine were Acts of Service and Words of Affirmation, while Greg's were Physical Touch and Quality Time. The results seemed so obvious that we couldn't believe we needed a quiz to prove them! But now that they were written in black and white, the hard work to actually apply this knowledge needed to begin.

We quickly realized that we were each trying to show love in the way we wanted to receive it. It's a common misunderstanding, but one that led us down a rabbit hole of resentment and frustration. But now that we understood what the other needed, we looked for opportunities to make small changes. Instead of trying to make Greg feel loved by doing things *for* him (how I felt loved), I focused on doing things *with* him (the way he felt loved). I'll admit it felt insincere at first. I didn't quite understand how or why it meant anything to him. But then I realized that whether or not I understood wasn't the point. Questioning him over why he found it more loving to be greeted with a hug than if he walked into a clean home was a way of judging his needs. The choice wasn't mine to make. Or change. Or withhold. It was for me to validate. The same was true for him. If he wanted me to feel loved and supported when I'm feeling stressed, cuddling wasn't going to cut it. But diving into the dishes would. Complimenting me and acknowledging the work I'm doing also would.

Doing things based on each other's love language felt kind of forced at first, but it paid off. Are there still times we miss? Yep. Have our love languages ever changed? Yep. But it all started with opening ourselves up enough to make room for each other's needs.

Daily communication, being vulnerable, understanding the other's love language—these are all vital in building a more durable and connected relationship. But there's still one essential piece that's missing, and that's sex. And while all of the things I just listed did help to improve our sense of intimacy, there were still conversations Greg and I needed to have about ourselves and each other when it came to sex.

As much as we all want to have a great sex life with our mate, it can be really difficult to talk about. Getting on the same page is something we want to just magically happen rather than having to work to get there. Sharing past experiences, insecurities, and beliefs around it can feel like a minefield. As Greg and I shared more of ourselves, it didn't take long to realize how much we'd been keeping from one another on issues related to being intimate. For one thing, I'd never revealed to Greg how tangled up sex was with my own self-worth and sense of shame. And he'd never shared with me just how rejected he felt as a husband and a man when I wasn't in the mood. Add in our different love languages and it's no wonder our sex life was suffering!

We had to get real about our beliefs and biases around sex. In our work, we shared past experiences and confronted feelings of shame and negativity around being intimate. I worked to detach my self-worth with sex and (finally) reject all of the societal messages that influenced my feelings about it. It allowed me to develop a healthier and more positive view of my own sexuality. And my being honest with Greg about this work also helped me realize that he'd moved way past his rock star phase. In fact, I may have projected onto him how "rockin'" his rock star phase actually was. So between my own newfound security and my trust in him, I could let go of my anxieties around being *enough* for him.

Greg's work entailed decoupling his worth as a man and husband from our sex life. Doing this helped him realize that my not being in the mood had nothing to do with my feelings about him as a person. Nor did it mean I no longer desired or loved him.

Learning all of this about each other helped both of us feel seen and loved, which created such an incredible feeling of intimacy. It opened us up to exploring ways to enrich our sex life together. This ranged from trying new things in the bedroom to simply spending more quality time together outside of sex. By prioritizing intimacy and connection in and out of the bedroom, we were able to deepen our bond and develop a more fulfilling relationship.

Keep in mind a relationship is a living thing. It changes as you do. It needs constant attention but it's often, unfortunately, the thing we back-burner when life's other needs arise. But the great thing about all of this work is that you can (and should) come back to it whenever you need to. And when it's done with commitment and honesty, it should result in a union that's not only more fulfilling but also more malleable, so that when life does get in the way, your relationship doesn't have to suffer.

HIT THE RESET BUTTON ON YOUR RELATIONSHIP

During the Reflection

Are you working as team?
Be honest: Are you and your partner more scorekeepers than team builders? If the "me versus you" dynamic felt relatable, then it's time to reassess how and why you and your partner "get" what you want. Remember, triggers don't always mean your partner did something wrong; it simply means that something feels unresolved. Dig in to discover the why first, then bring it to your partner.

How are you showing up to your relationship?
Take a moment to evaluate your communication patterns and whether you act out of fear or love. Do you allow "shoulds" and shame to interfere with your connection with your partner? Do you project feelings onto your partner in an effort to protect yourself? Are you showing up to each moment with a scoreless, clean slate, open and ready for deeper connection? By owning your presence and contribution to the relationship, you can begin to uncover and break through stale patterns and communication rituals.

What are ways that you feel loved? What are ways your partner feels loved?
Observe the behaviors and gestures you make toward each other. The way these specific actions or words resonate with you can give you clues about your primary love languages. Does your partner jump for joy when you bring them a surprise gift or do they prefer a flirtatious text? Do you feel extra loved when

your partner gives you a long hug or does a chore do it for you? Greg and I learned more by reading the book and taking the online Love Languages quiz to help us identify our languages. While doing this together is ideal, you can totally complete this individually to gain more insight about yourself.

What does intimacy mean to you? To your partner?
As with love languages, intimacy can mean different things to different people. For a long time, intimacy to me was synonymous with sex. And because my experience with sex was more of a duty or validation of my desirability, I was completely closed off to the idea of emotional closeness and connection. Have you ever stopped to consider what intimacy means to you and your partner? Are you taking the time to acknowledge the little gestures that show you your partner cares? Or are you staying busy with distractions and avoiding intimacy altogether?

Are you having honest conversations, even uncomfortable ones?
It's inevitable. Challenging topics about family dynamics, finances, and your emotions will present themselves in your relationship. Over and over and over again. Avoiding difficult conversations is like sweeping dirt under a rug; it may make the surface look clean, but the mess of misunderstandings and resentment will still be there, waiting to be dealt with. Are you creating a safe and nonjudgmental space for your partner to share their thoughts and feelings? Do you feel safe expressing your own? Are you willing to listen with an open mind and without defensiveness? Are you being honest, even when it hurts?

During the Reset

Invite your marriage into the relationship.
Oh hey! There's a third party to this union and it's called the Marriage. When two individuals come together in marriage, they create a unique entity that has its own set of needs, desires, and challenges. When both partners view the marriage as an entity in itself, they can make decisions that benefit the relationship as a whole, rather than just their individual needs.

Treat your relationship as a privilege rather than as an obligation.
Here's a little dose of relationship wisdom that has really helped me: Shift your perspective from "I have to" to "I get to." You don't *have* to go on date nights or surprise your partner with thoughtful gestures, you *get* to! Relationships are voluntary and that goes both ways. Remember those qualities that once made your heart flutter with excitement? Funny how we can become annoyed by the very same traits we were initially attracted to. So, take a step back and remind yourself of the reasons you fell in love. Embrace the quirks, the imperfections, and the little idiosyncrasies that make your partner who they are.

Focus your effort on showing love in the language your partner understands.
Step one was understanding how you each feel loved. But, instead of getting caught up in your own love lingo, focus on *speaking* theirs. Sure, it may feel awkward or forced at first, but that's just because you're used to speaking your own language. And remember, there's no need to judge their language. It isn't for you to project your feelings onto. Just keep at it, and before you know it, you'll be fluent.

Create opportunities for intimacy.
I've learned that it's important to define intimacy, embrace it, and stop avoiding it like the plague. I've also learned that it doesn't just happen, it takes effort to keep it in focus. Initially, I found it challenging to open up emotionally, while Greg struggled to recognize and honor small gestures that weren't sexual. By paying attention to intimacy of all types—emotional, physical, mental, sexual, and spiritual—there is opportunity to recognize effort and create moments that may otherwise be overlooked.

Commit to a check-in.
It doesn't have to be a fancy date night; it can be as simple as a daily or even weekly conversation about whether each other's needs are being met or have changed. It might feel odd at first, but it's not meant to be some formal conversation. Just take each other's temperature. Greg and I make time for this as we walk our pup or as we shut down the day. Don't forget to ask for feedback on how you're doing! And if you find that you need some extra support, consider seeking the guidance of a therapist to help navigate any challenges that may arise.

During the Reinvention

A stronger connection equals less friction.
By actively listening and seeking to understand each other's perspectives, you avoid jumping to solutions or blaming each other. Prioritizing support and continuing to find new ways to work toward common goals brings you closer together. And why not spice things up by reading some books on communication and connection together? It's like doing maintenance on your relationship, and who doesn't love a well-oiled machine?

Cultivate gratitude and respect.
When you approach your relationship as a privilege, it adds a sprinkle of gratitude and a pinch of playfulness that can breathe new life into your connection. It's important to remember to continue finding ways to honor your partner and the marriage itself—especially as you evolve individually and as seasons in your life change. By doing so, you can maintain the positive energy and continue to deepen your connection and respect toward each other.

Give more, expect less.
Our brains are wired for reciprocity, so when we give with kindness, love, and generosity, the chances are high that it will be returned. It's not about giving to receive but rather giving freely and authentically. Coincidentally, when I started giving to Greg without keeping score or having any expectation of anything in return, it also made me feel more love toward myself.

Increased intimacy reduces the stress and strain on the relationship.
When you ramp up the intimacy in all aspects of your relationship, you'll experience strengthened trust and confidence. This forms a solid foundation where both partners feel safe and supported. You'll be better equipped to handle conflicts and difficulties, knowing that you have a reliable and understanding partner by your side.

Meet your partner where they are.
Maintaining a strong relationship requires embracing each other's journey without expectations of progress, speed, or readiness. By continuously accepting and supporting each other's individual paths of self-discovery, you foster a healthier and more harmonious relationship dynamic.

SECTION 3

Resetting How You Deal with Your Shit...
Toxic Coping Strategies

INTRODUCTION

RESETTING HOW YOU DEAL WITH YOUR SHIT

Initial Thoughts

How do you deal with your shit? How do you deal when you're feeling shitty? Overwhelmed? Anxious? We all have coping mechanisms, whether we're conscious of them or not. Often they're based on examples from our childhood that we mirror once we're adults. Or they're in opposition to what we observed as children, not necessarily because they're better, but because they're different from what our parents did. Learning how to cope is often based on experience rather than any substantive guidance. Yet, unhealthy coping tools can be disruptive and stall growth in every area of our life. This was certainly true for me. That's why my book and my story would be nothing without this section.

If you're anything like I was, how you get through daily stresses is not something you think much about. Indeed, unless your strategies are glaringly "bad," what's the harm? There is so much more in everyday life that needs thinking about and tackling. If having a drink, shopping, scouring social media, et cetera, helps get you through, then what's the difference? Questioning things means rocking the boat, and who has time for that? Especially if there's no guarantee that your metaphorical boat might not sink in the process. Then years pass and you've never examined whether those strategies serve you or, worse, have hindered you along the way.

Change is petrifying. Dealing with our shit and owning our circumstances as a result of our choices is painful. My way of coping was all about distraction and subterfuge. I didn't want to investigate and shine a light on my feelings; I was too worried about what I'd unearth. I believed my coping tools made me happy. It flooded my body with enough dopamine to get me through and put a smile on my face. For a long time, I believed that was enough. In truth, I believed that was all I deserved.

I've made it pretty clear in previous chapters that drinking and even sometimes drugs were my strategies for dealing with life. Yet, I never considered myself to be an addict—not in the physiological sense. I could stop without shakes, without detoxing. So that meant that using substances to deal with my life was okay, right? (Cue a side-eye glance here.) What about the gossipaholic—we all know one—that person who can't stop talking about other people's problems and issues so they never really have to investigate their own? Or the friend who finds refuge in shopping for things they don't need? The truth is, whether it's alcohol, binge eating, or simply hiding under the covers and retreating, challenging yourself to examine whether your strategies are truly helping you cope is a worthy exercise. It certainly was for me.

That's why, in this section, I share my own personal experience with alcohol: the process of evaluating its place in my life and its impact. Why had I accepted it as a normal, often daily, indulgence? What was I trying so hard to avoid? And, coincidentally, how was it numbing me from feeling positive things as well?

As you read this, I invite you to replace my experience with alcohol with your coping mechanism of choice. When I share my lack of awareness about the dangerous situations I was constantly finding myself in, consider the dangers associated with your tactic. For example, if shopping is your way to procrastinate, avoid difficult situations, or distract your mind, are you creating danger in your financial wellness or relationship categories?

Let's take a deep dive into our behavior, the things that are keeping us from being the best version of ourselves. The truth is, there is a ton of denial about these things. A ton of rationalization. A ton of excuses and blame. But every part of personal growth and meaningful change pivots on digging into this. It can be the most challenging and darkest part of growth. There will be hard lessons and missteps. However, as you shed these old habits, you connect with yourself and your motivation more intimately, enriching every facet of your life—in ways you could never imagine. You approach daily stresses with a sense of readiness rather than from a reactionary crouch. From discovering opportunities to experiencing an overwhelming sense of self-reliance, self-worth, and calm—this work is one of the greatest gifts you can give yourself.

You're worth it.

RESETTING HOW YOU DEAL WITH YOUR SHIT

Coping Habits

Within a week or so of Greg discovering my affair, I found myself humbly and nervously entering an NA meeting. I very hesitantly went at the suggestion of a wonderful friend whose own life had been profoundly improved by Narcotics Anonymous. This is not something I ever would have considered seeking out on my own or would have thought was necessary, but he posited that maybe it was an addiction to attention that caused me to risk my home and relationship, and I was self-aware enough to know that I couldn't deny my longing for the spotlight. It was also true that, similar to other addictions, my need for attention caused increasingly riskier behaviors up and until I was found out. I can still remember those quick hits of dopamine rushing through my system during my affair. I often even compared the feeling to needing a fix or to being high, so when the suggestion was made, it wasn't hard to find the parallels between myself and someone who was addicted to drugs. And frankly, I would've done just about anything to prove to Greg that I wanted our marriage to survive. So off I went to NA.

The Reset Button

Walking into that room that day, I genuinely hoped that I could find some answers to the big WHY? Why did I do this? Why did I have this need? Was this the place to find those answers? I wasn't sure. I was also flooded with feelings of imposter syndrome. Though I saw the commonalities between myself and substance abusers, I wasn't confident that others would agree. My friend assured me that I would be welcomed there, but I was still incredibly nervous. But as it turned out, he was right. I was embraced without question. And though I was so wrapped up in the turbulence of my own problems to have any real expectations of what (and who) I'd find at this meeting, what I discovered was that it was a microcosm of the outside world. Some of the attendees were social; some preferred to be alone. Some were there because the court required it, while others came of their own volition. But much of the energy in that room matched my own: a mixture of anxiety, hopefulness, circumspection, and contrition.

The meeting began with the Serenity Prayer.

> *God, grant me the serenity*
> *to accept the things I cannot change;*
> *courage to change the things I can;*
> *and wisdom to know the difference.*

As I listened to its words, I suddenly understood something that was integral to opening a door to growth. It was that at this point in my life, I had absolutely no understanding of myself. For me, this epiphany was huge. Admitting such a thing required a kind of surrendering I'd never been able to do before. I was always driven to be the best at everything that meant anything to me. So the idea that I didn't know or understand something or that I would willingly concede feelings of insecurity was radical to me. But as the meeting continued and I listened to one brave soul after another share their story, I was surprised to find that

I recognized myself in them. Over and over again. There was so much pain, so much struggle, so much familiarity. And for what was probably the first time in my life, I saw vulnerability as strength. I saw the bravery in confessing that something was difficult or uncomfortable. How revealing the challenge only emboldened their conviction and commitment to remaining sober. And how bettering their lives meant having to actually embrace their feelings. It was a profound experience that I will always be grateful for.

As much gratitude as I had for going to that meeting, and I had a lot, I never returned to NA or worked the twelve steps. I couldn't shake the feeling that I didn't belong there. I was ashamed of the mess that I'd made of my life all on my own. In short, I felt too guilty to return.

Back then, it never occurred to me that some people's reliance on substances mirrored my own need for alcohol. I was so focused on my affair, my "issues," that it never occurred to me to investigate my own coping mechanisms or, frankly, even acknowledge that I had any. For me, alcohol was just always there. It was so integrated into my life—from childhood to adulthood—that I never questioned its reason for being there.

From the time I was a teenager, drinking was a huge part of my life. Actually, it was a huge part of my identity. Though I didn't realize it at the time, interwoven in most of my decisions, my activities, and even my inner narrative were thoughts about my next drink. We often think of the dangers of using alcohol to cope with challenges, which I definitely did, but there's also a lot of risk when it's your go-to way of celebrating, of relaxing, and of socializing—of associating drinking with every part of your life. And I did. Drinking was so second nature in my life and surrounding environment that it never occurred to me to stop. Once our couples counselor merely suggested that Greg and I stop drinking for a while, and we were like, "What? Are pigs flying outside?" Even the idea felt ridiculous. Who doesn't drink?

Growing up, I never thought twice about seeing my parents and their friends with a glass of something in their hands. I remember our neighbor often having a beer ready for my dad when he came home from work. And as an adult, my friends and I mirrored that same behavior by turning get-togethers into a kind of happy hour. Drinking was synonymous with adulting. Many days of the week we would gather at someone's house at 3 PM (or earlier, ahem) to watch the kids and drink from coffee mugs brimming with wine. Adulting!

It's not only that alcohol was just around; I also internalized that choosing not to drink meant you were a goody-goody or boring. I can't quite remember where that narrative originated from, but I think it was likely from listening to the older teenagers in my childhood orbit. I remember looking forward to drinking when I was "old enough," which meant when I was a teenager (though I dabbled when I was even younger). I wanted to be cool and rebellious. I thought it was the perfect accompaniment to my being a good athlete, straight A student, and musician. It was my way of hitting all the popular kid marks: the one who could be the life of the party while maintaining the "good kid" cred. Moving through the different cliques—the partyers, the studiers, the athletes, and so on—meant that I could claim a space with everyone and was free from forcing any one identity on myself. I was "cool" like that. I savored the kind of power and popularity it provided.

Once I anointed myself old enough to handle alcohol, I began slipping in and out of the house without being noticed. As I mentioned in previous chapters, my partying happened to coincide with my parents' divorce, so they had a lot going on both emotionally and logistically. The timing of their divorce also helped me learn how to push down my feelings one shot at a time. I began making a habit of finding distractions (good and bad ones) to keep my mind off of my feelings. From high school to college and well into adulthood, much of my time was spent perfecting a vicious cycle of drinking. It started with gaining social acceptance and praise for being fun, moved into losing my inhibitions, which inevitably led to my making terrible and even dangerous choices, then making excuses and apologies for said decisions, and finally to feeling palpable regret and embarrassment. It was my Saturday (and Thursday and Friday) special. Alcohol and partying allowed me to connect and disconnect at the same time. Getting plastered also happens to be the greatest scapegoat in the world. It was like a permission slip to be as bad as I wanted. It didn't matter that my guilt and shame over my behavior was compounding with every night out. And as those negative feelings became more entrenched and as my problems became more adult, I only grew more devoted to using alcohol to cope.

In Ohio, Greg and I had great groups of friends to socialize with: friends from back home, band friends, neighborhood friends, and so on. We drank with all of them! And by "drank," I mean that they drank while Greg and I very often got hammered. Nobody could hold a candle to our commitment to having a good time. As I mentioned previously, when Greg drank, he transformed into an entertainer: one part stand-up comic, one part musician. When I drank, it was like I morphed into the all-powerful Oz of partying. It was not simply that I lost inhibitions; it was that I pushed everyone else to lose theirs as well. And, as you know from previous mentions, apologizing for saying or doing something over the line became so common that Greg and I coined a phrase for it: the Sunday Sorrys. Sometimes I had to apologize for making people feel uncomfortable, like when I hosted a surprise thirtieth birthday party for Greg and I got loaded and decided to remove my pants. Sure, I was wearing a long tunic, but it wasn't quite long enough to wear with only underwear. But I didn't stop there. I proceeded to give all of the guests (including my brother-in-law) shots accompanied with a lap dance. At my own bachelorette party I got so drunk and mean that I cussed everyone out and passed out with a bottle of Jäger outside the front door of my friend's condo. I've been in bar fights. I've broken friends' things (and then not even offered to replace them). And I was almost arrested more than once for peeing in public. But again, I had the Sunday Sorrys to show my contrition and wipe the slate clean for the next weekend.

Over the years, Greg and I got an inkling that some friends had withdrawn from hanging out with us. In fact, we recently found out from a couple that we've known for years that they distanced themselves from us because not only did we want to keep the party going beyond reason, we also had a habit of drunkenly arguing as well. For us, blowing off steam didn't only mean having a great time; it also meant airing out our grievances with each other—in public. Nobody wants to go out for a fun night with friends only to be forced to play audience to a grudge match. So they understandably started socializing with us less. Other friends withdrew because Greg and I were so aggressive in our efforts to keep everyone drinking. We didn't care that they wanted to be able to function the next day without a hangover pressing down on them. We lived for the party and believed that everyone else needed to do the same. In the end, I think for some of our social circle, it just became easier to avoid going out with us than it was to have to deal with the pressure of saying no to yet another round of shots.

Drinking grew into something that was beyond letting my hair down. Something in me needed a metaphorical hall pass to do whatever I wanted without claiming ownership over any of it. As I said, it was the perfect scapegoat. With each drink, I happily allowed my moral compass and boundaries to dissolve. And as I grew into the number one partyer, the queen of the last call, I became so aligned with that identity that I worried that stepping down from my party perch would reveal that behind my loud mouth was only smoke and mirrors—or worse, someone boring! But this insecurity was deeply buried and it would take much more time and self-discovery to realize it. In Ohio, I was steadfast in my belief that drinking was the solution to all things good and bad.

You might be wondering why, at that Narcotics Anonymous meeting, it never occurred to me that I might have had an unhealthy relationship with alcohol. The truth is, it didn't. Besides the fact that realizing that would have required a lot more introspection than I was ready for, my drinking—the reasons I drank, when I drank, and even how much I drank—wasn't so different from everyone else around me. Sure, I could drink most of my friends and family under the table, but I chalked that up to my being so committed to all of my endeavors. If I wanted to let loose, I wanted to be the best at it, dammit! But it was never hard to find friends to join me for a glass of liquid courage, a flute of celebration, or a toast to the fact that it was Friday (or any day on the calendar!). Added to that was the fact that I was always able to stop when there was something more important going on in my life, like a pregnancy or training for a competition. Surely if I relied on getting loaded in order to live my life, I wouldn't be able to just stop like that, right? So, as you know, I kept the party going.

Fast-forward to our move to Florida and to Greg's decision to stop drinking. When Greg decides something, a whole lot of determination goes along with it. That helped him with his commitment, because it was a huge lifestyle change. Not only for us as a couple but also in his professional life. He quickly realized just how many events coincided with drinking, so early on in the first month or so, there were some knuckle-through moments. Happy hours with his new colleagues were pretty challenging— like social anxiety and the sweats challenging—but he got through it. Eventually he just changed his people, places, and things. Actually, *we* did. It also helped that we hadn't really established ourselves socially or professionally in Florida yet. We were still so raw as a couple that we weren't in a hurry to make friends or be around a ton of people all the time.

I chose to support Greg's decision to live a sober life by not drinking when he was around. This meant that for about six months, I was basically living a sober life as well. But then I got a new job with the Discovery Education team and my life (and lifestyle) shifted tremendously.

When Greg and I made the move to Florida, we were both grateful to have jobs waiting for us. But not long into our new life, both of us were feeling dissatisfied professionally. Greg made the brave decision to go out on his own and start a mortgage business. It was a big risk, but one that I admired. I, too, was miserable at work. Between the long commute, the constraints of the industry, and feeling rushed all the freaking time, I needed to figure out an exit plan. I decided to start with something I truly loved—fitness. So, with my bodybuilding coach's support, I posted a video offering fitness and nutrition planning. It allowed me to indulge my passion and explore a possible side hustle. I called it Cameo Fitness and almost immediately started signing clients. Soon after, a friend from college saw the videos and was so impressed by them that he contacted me to gauge my interest in a sales job on his Discovery Education team (at the Discovery Network). I had to turn it down because the role was back in Ohio but, coincidentally, his sister, who managed a team in Florida, also had an opening. I quickly put together a presentation, flew to Discovery's offices in Chicago for my interview, and landed the job. The salary was double what I was making at the bank and even included a generous bonus. The opportunity felt serendipitous because it not only allowed me the chance to try something new, it also gave us more of a financial cushion as Greg got his business off the ground. And a big ol' cushion was definitely required. Remember all of that credit card debt we had? Well, it was still there, so I had to have a steady income while Greg worked on building his network from scratch. The new gig required a lot of traveling for me, but since Greg was working from home, he was in charge of his schedule and could more easily manage things with the kids.

Two weeks after Discovery offered me the position, I began my new career selling professional development and technology programs to school districts in Florida and Louisiana. I traveled regularly in order to meet with superintendents, attend symposiums, visit school districts, and take part in meetings at Discovery headquarters in Chicago and DC. I had a great team and I was energized by the new opportunity. I also had a lot of confidence in my sales skills. However, I was insecure about my lack of education. There I was, a college dropout, selling educational programs. I knew I was bright and I was confident in my understanding of what I was selling, but I couldn't escape my feelings of inadequacy when it came to my background. With no degree to tout, I leaned on my social acumen instead. My clients wouldn't question my authority on subjects if they were having too good of a time during our meetings. And for me, good times equated drinking. Suddenly I was back to some of my old behaviors, albeit in more professional settings. I certainly wasn't taking my pants off, but I was pushing the envelope for client dinners and team meetings. It started with my first outing with the Discovery Education team. They ordered drinks, so I did as well: a vodka tonic. Fine. But then the next day, when we went out again, I ordered a margarita and three fingers of whiskey, which, I told myself, was only to fight a sore throat, and egged everyone else on to order a round of shots. I can recall everyone looking at me like, "whoa, okay!" I wanted to succeed and, ironically, I wanted to be taken seriously as a vital team player, and getting everyone soused and having a good time was my way of doing it. Things continued this way on work trips. The table would start with individual glasses of wine and then I'd keep filling people's glasses. Then I'd return home from my travels and go back to sober living.

For a while, I thought I was managing my two different lifestyles well—until I was at a team outing in Chicago. My coworkers and I were closing down a busy week at a Friday happy hour. Greg had flown to Chicago to meet me and was on his way to the bar. I had just poured my second or third glass of wine—a very generous pour—when I saw him walking up to the bar. I panicked. I chugged that glass of wine down as fast as I could so that I could get it all before he entered the bar. After I swallowed the last of it down, I realized how crazy that was. Greg knew I was still drinking and he never asked me not to drink in front of him, but it was important to me that I didn't. But I very well could have handed that glass of wine to a friend. Instead, I needed desperately to finish it—every last drop. That's when I realized that my relationship to drinking wasn't what I wanted it to be. In fact, in that moment, I realized I didn't want a relationship with it at all. I never wanted to feel that sense of panic ever again. And that was the last drink I've ever had.

It's been about ten years since that glass of wine. I'll admit, at the bar that night, I didn't use the words *never again*. I was too afraid to put that kind of pressure on myself. But as the days, weeks, and years went by and I grew more accustomed and comfortable with situations sans alcohol, it just got easier. And better. And richer. But it unearthed so much inside of me that I had no idea was buried. With no alcohol, I had no choice but to deal with it.

RESETTING HOW YOU DEAL WITH YOUR SHIT

Doing It One Day at a Time

Ten years. As I write this, I'm still amazed that it's been nearly a decade since I caught myself downing a glass of wine as if it were a shot. But, as I said, I didn't make some sweeping grand decision. Instead, I decided not to drink for an entire day.

The day after that, I made a conscious choice to continue not drinking for that day as well.

And again the day after that.

And so on.

I clung to ideas like "one day at a time" and "just for today, I'm not drinking." This allowed the time to pass without feeling the weight of "never again" hanging over me. The weeks went by. Then months. And soon it all added up to years. A decade. Even though, day after day, I reaffirmed my choice to live a sober life, I still told myself the decision was temporary. After all, everything was temporary, right? So that also applied to abstaining from drinking. Thinking that way helped tremendously.

Not surprisingly, there were many days that simply deciding not to drink wasn't enough to carry me through. Drinking was like swimming with those floaties that keep babies safely on the surface of the water. Without it, I flailed at first, sometimes grasping for something to grab on to. Sometimes I didn't want to deal with it at all—like the days I stayed in bed. My reflex was to seek out other crutches, like smoking, or any careless habit that helped me circumvent my feelings. But with every sober day, my need for "floaties" lessened. I wouldn't go so far as to say it disappeared, but I was starting to swim on my own. And as I successfully managed to move through each day without alcohol, I had the proof I needed that I could function without it. With that came the realization that I had confidence and courage—the authentic kind, not the liquid stuff.

My priority pyramid also helped in my sober pursuits. When I considered what things and which people were most important to me, it was clear that there was no space for alcohol or irresponsible partying. Truthfully, this realization might not have occurred had we still been living in Ohio. I had such a solid support system there and so many people I could rely on if I needed to go out and blow off steam or if I was too hungover to function.

All that familiarity gave me the protection I needed when I made terrible, alcohol-fueled choices. Finding myself in a dangerous situation didn't have the shock waves of consequences in Ohio that they would in Florida, because there was always a crew of people to cover for me. I think about the situations I got myself into back then and can't imagine what would've happened had they occurred while I was in this new place with no real community to rely on. I think about the time Greg was performing at an outdoor festival and I got totally loaded. We got into a huge argument about who-knows-what, and he left me there. Since familiar faces surrounded me and I was too drunk to give a damn, I didn't care that I was stranded. I kept partying and socializing. Did I mention that my cell phone had died too? That I had no money? No ID? Late into the night, I drunkenly wandered barefoot to the after-party, my high heel shoes slung over my shoulder. I'd stumble into strangers on the sidewalk, linking into their arms so I could do-si-do with them. Not a care in the world! To this day, I have no idea how I got to my destination, and I bristle when I think about what could have happened.

Similar to that was when I was at a bachelorette party in Columbus, a place I knew like the back of my hand. The party however, included a number of women I didn't know—even the host. Once at the bar, I was too busy getting annihilated and mingling to notice that the group was leaving. Eventually I realized I was alone and stuck. Again, my cell phone battery was dead. I knew the group returned to the host's house, but I didn't know where that was because I didn't know her. But, as happens when you've lived somewhere all your life, I ran into an old friend and crashed at his house for the night. Ohio, for me, was like the protective padding you wear when you're playing sports, and I took advantage of it.

In Florida, aftershocks of getting pulled over or getting into trouble were guaranteed. We didn't even have a babysitter yet, no less someone to call if I needed rescuing. My in-laws weren't local anymore, so they couldn't entertain my kids while I sacked out on the couch for the day because of an epic hangover. There was no one to bail us out, no one to stand in for us, no one to save us. Greg and I both had no choice but to take ownership over our choices. After a while of doing that, I realized just how much time I gave over to other people when it came to my kids. It makes me so sad. Then again, when I was in the midst of it, it seemed normal.

Life without alcohol makes you realize how often adults are confronted with it. Samples of wine come at you in the grocery store. Servers angle for you to make your virgin cocktail "adult." Even situations that are about or for kids, like birthday parties or playdates, are also about imbibing. I happily took part in this ritual. I remember being at my kids' games and getting my buzz on as I sipped from my Yeti. Alcohol is always there, whether in the background or the star of the show. That made it hard sometimes, especially if I was feeling vulnerable or reminiscent about my liquid wingman. Truthfully, I missed some of the fun of it—and I'd be lying if I didn't say that it could be fun. Granted, I had a habit of taking the fun way, way too far, but I missed how it loosened me up.

I will say that there was one bonus of having alcohol thrust in my face so often. It brought out my rebellious side. My need to feel like I lived against the grain—that I was my own person. Maybe everyone was drinking at this event, but I wasn't everyone. That really appealed to me. I felt empowered by the feeling of control it gave me. It was a type of control I hadn't seen many examples of in my life.

Telling people you don't drink is an interesting kind of social experiment. Generally speaking, I've noticed that Greg and I usually get one of two responses. The first is disbelief: *You don't ever drink?* And I totally get this reaction. It's one that I probably would have had when I was still drinking. As I mentioned earlier, it took me a long time to realize that not drinking was even an option, so this incredulousness makes sense to me. The second response that we typically get is one of self-reflection. People instinctually want to qualify when and how much alcohol they consume. Whether it's from some deep shame on their part, some fear of being judged by us, or a way for them to try to connect with our life choice, I have no idea. It used to make us both feel like we needed to offer some explanation for our decision. I'd mollify their discomfort by sharing that I wasn't a "good "drinker, that one was never enough for me, or that it no longer fit into the life that Greg and I were leading. It took a while to realize that this was really nobody's business and that it wasn't my job to make other people comfortable with my choices. Neither Greg nor I judge anyone else's way of life. So there was no reason for me to act as if others were in judgment of mine.

The people who knew us in Ohio, both family and friends, understandably had mixed reactions when they found out that we had stopped drinking. Shock was one. Belief that our choice was a fad or phase or even a joke was another. In fairness to them, this was quite a leap from who they knew us to be when we lived in Ohio. It's understandable that it took them a minute to reset. Some friendships, the ones that were solely based around partying, naturally withered away. It was sad but not surprising. Many of our relationships, though, grew much deeper. Even though we see our Ohio friends only once or twice a year, there are some friendships that are so much more profound now. Regardless of the miles between us, when we get together now, we really get together. And although this was never our purpose, some friends mentioned to us that our sobriety made them consider and reevaluate their own.

Both my and Greg's parents have been incredibly supportive as well. They've seen how much growth Greg and I have achieved as a direct result of not drinking. For a while, they all felt bashful about drinking in front of us, but they have since learned that Greg and I truly don't care.

As it happened, the timing of my last drink came just before summer break. We were celebrating the one-year anniversary of our move to Florida. It was around then that we started branching out socially as well. Greg and I happened to become close with another couple that weren't formally sober but barely drank. This meant that for the first time, we were creating friendships that weren't based around getting loaded. They liked us for us and we liked them for them. I didn't always have to have my party face on when we got together. I felt relief in that. It was the first time in a long time that I was making real friendships without a shared interest in getting plastered. It was also the first time that I didn't try to *be* something for them—the outrageous friend, the one who turns every get-together into *the best time*, the mascot for fun—I was just whoever I felt like on that day. Sometimes I was still really fun and funny, but other days when we saw them I was honest about being exhausted from work or frustrated with the kids. I also had to own who I was socially. For example, if I went out and gossiped, I didn't have the bottle of wine to blame. Afterward I'd ask myself whether that was who I wanted to be. And if it was, why? How did that serve me? When I was drinking, these questions never arose, because I'd always scapegoat the alcohol. I'm not bitchy; the tequila is. I wouldn't have shared that person's secret were it not for that fifth shot of whiskey… I had to own my choices and take responsibility for them.

I know I mentioned previously that taking the alcohol away from date nights with Greg allowed us to connect more fully, but, boy, in the beginning, it sure was nerve-wracking. Sober dating began before I stopping drinking because I wanted to support Greg's decision to live alcohol-free. But early on in Florida, our relationship was so rocky that denying my margarita reflex was challenging. Yes, we had agreed to be less judgmental and more vulnerable with one another, but saying it and doing it are not the same. And virgin cocktails are no match for the fear that dating while on the wagon might mean you don't like each other as much as you thought you did. I'll admit there were nights I would silently pine for that jazzy feeling that would run through me with my first drink. The lubrication would open up conversation and make the evening feel easier. Once taken away, I had to trust that he and I, as ourselves, were enough to make the evening fun.

Even the sex was different at first. Sober sex was like doing it with a spotlight on you—especially for me. Everything felt new and slightly off. Not bad, but off. Almost robotic. When my brain was bathed in alcohol I could drown out all of my inhibitions and insecurities—about my body, about whether I could keep Greg satisfied, and about whether I could stand up to his past lovers. Being drunk made me carefree, and it took time to find my way there without that crutch. Without liquid courage, all of those little tormenting voices were center stage, keeping me from being fully engaged and enjoying what I was actually doing. It seemed that everywhere I turned I was faced with only one choice: to be vulnerable and honest. So, I had to learn to face my fear of intimacy and inadequacy and trust that removing alcohol would open up a deeper level of connection.

Within a couple of weeks of my "unknown last" drink, Greg and I went to our first alcohol-free music festival for a weekend. The idea would have seemed radical in our previous life! But there we were, doing something we both loved—listening to music—without our crutch. We drank lemon shake ups and ate kettle corn and people watched. At some point during the weekend, we realized we were having a blast. We were connecting, clear-eyed and joyful. And afterward, we remembered every moment and every band we saw. While it was weird not to be double fisting drinks and getting so loaded that we ended up screaming at each other by night's end, it was probably the first time we realized that if we could manage not drinking in a setting like that, then we could do it anywhere. When the weekend ended, it was nice to be able to look back on it without trepidation. To have a shared experience with my husband that was about the event and not about how we behaved. Greg loved that too. It made us finally admit something we'd always kind of known: that one drink was too many and a thousand would never be enough, so leaving it behind was the only way to live.

You know what else not drinking allowed me? Time! Partying the way I did and getting hammered as often as I was getting hammered took a lot of time. If I wasn't hungover to the point of being utterly useless the next day, I was usually still exhausted from the very late night. Between work, the kids, and my social life, I had little time or energy left to do anything that enriched me. You can't really think deeply about your life goals when your head feels like someone is putting a chain saw to it. If the thought of brewing a pot of coffee makes you want to go back to bed, then you definitely don't have the energy to journal your way out of some complicated feelings. With the absence of blowing off steam, I suddenly had the space for other things I loved, like playing music. Considering the huge part that music played in our life, Greg never realized until we were sober that he'd married a musician. All that childhood training I'd gotten was still there, but I was too busy dancing on the tables or making a show of drunkenly stealing the spotlight that he never took my musical abilities seriously. But showing off my musical chops while being stone-cold sober meant that Greg and I found another way to connect with each other. And because we were also working better as a team, my playing music with him didn't make him feel territorial or make me feel like we were in competition with one another. It was something we could share and appreciate in one another.

In addition to dealing with the adjustment of relating to the world and people around me, I also had to adapt to how I dealt with myself and my feelings. All the other times I had stopped drinking, I had no intention of quitting altogether. It was for an external reason: I was pregnant; I was training. Once that reason was no longer present, I'd take drinking right back up again. So I never had to learn how to deal with my thoughts and feelings. Or myself. Getting drunk was my outlet. But now that I had no expiration date to my sobriety, I had to accept that actually processing my feelings would be the only outlet I had left. I had to figure out how to settle into my emotions—the good and the "bad" ones. I needed to turn inward, find acceptance, and foster love and compassion for myself. As you can imagine, this was not always easy. There were things about myself that I hated having to confront—parts of myself that made me *want* to drink. Sure, blowing off steam from a hard week is fun, but what really made me order shots was when certain parts of myself got triggered. They'd rear their ugly heads and my instinct was to drown them away. Send them down a river of whiskey. Or tequila.

Over time I've learned and had to parse through some of my alcohol triggers. My lack of body confidence was one. Feeling shame or embarrassment, that was another big one. Anytime I felt sad or uncomfortable with something that was happening in my life, I used the alcohol to push myself into an "I'm fine!" place. I also discovered how much I was trying to be socially acceptable. I was someone who was always comfortable with being alone. I never needed a huge group of friends, not in the way that Greg valued his circle of buddies. I thought that meant something was wrong with me. I drank so I could transform into the partyer, the one who seemed like the social butterfly (even though I was far from it). The truth was that I loved that Greg was my best friend and he was all I really needed. I don't mean to say that he was my everything, but he was always enough for me. When I stopped drinking, I learned how to feel okay with my lone wolf self. I stopped questioning whether it was socially acceptable because that no longer mattered.

Thankfully, by the time I was sober, I had already been doing a lot of work on myself. I had already started to bring movement and meditation into my daily life. I'd created my own mental safe space for feelings that made me uncomfortable. And so, taking my go-to escape away felt more like a natural step rather than like I was getting the rug pulled out from under me. But the transition was still rocky at times.

Amazingly, even when it got bumpy, this work felt liberating. The idea that I, Cameo the Imperfect, was enough was starting to take root. It was the perfect time to put down my Cameo the Partyer mask once and for all. I no longer needed it to feel worthy. And I stopped longing to numb out or escape. The transition felt so organic that I wonder if somewhere my brain knew I was ready to leave alcohol behind, and so as I downed that last glass of wine, I was able to see that action in a way I wouldn't have been able to before.

Ben was too young to remember a time when Greg and I were drinking, but Faith was nine years old when we quit. She definitely remembers the before and after. We've had honest conversations about those memories too. And... oof. She recalls the fighting, the hangovers, the general craziness of it all. She remembers a mostly disconnected mom who was not in touch with her emotions. A mom who was explosive and reactive. One who was angry a lot of the time. And, this is probably the hardest to admit, but she remembers not always feeling safe. Yes, this includes the incident with Greg and the night at the hotel, but there were other instances she mentioned as well. When she shared those memories, they were mostly of when I was acting reckless or out of control or just being too loud. I dismissed her initially. I told myself (and her) that they were just normal parts of life. I remember lacking empathy for her feelings. After all, there were so many similar recollections that mirrored Faith's from my own childhood. Wasn't it just a part of growing up? Maybe it was Faith who would need to toughen up in the same way I had to. Over time, I realized how wrong this was. It took a little bit, but I eventually validated her feelings and understood that just because I had similar memories of my own, it didn't mean that her emotions about them were wrong.

I'm grateful for the honest conversations she and I have been able to have around her experiences (even though they make me nauseated to think about). I remind myself that the benefit of her seeing the before and after is that she can truly understand the value of the work that Greg and I have put into ourselves and our family. We are more transparent and truthful now. Whereas before, if the kids were not listening or misbehaving, I would drink until I didn't care anymore, now I actually deal with it. It's hard, but because I confront it early on, I'm calmer, and because their behaviors are being addressed, the kids can actually account for their choices and learn something. It's not seamless or even pretty all the time, but it's honest. It's my hope that Faith and Ben habituate that way of living in the same way I habituated running away from my feelings.

Sometimes I think about what my life and my family would look like today if Greg and I made a different choice a decade ago. It would be so wildly different from what it is today. I guess, the better way to say it, is that it never would have changed. Greg and I would have kept bottling our feelings. Resenting each other. Blaming each other. We would have kept drinking and fighting and drinking and fighting and so on. More mess. More collateral damage. And our kids would have had very different parents— ones who were emotionally unavailable to them. I know this all sounds dramatic, but in looking back on who we were then, it's a pretty honest picture. Of course, had nothing changed, this picture would have given the appearance of a really good time, because Greg and I would have made a lot of friends in Florida that we could go out and party with. And how we appeared would have been more important than how we were.

I'm so glad we decided to deal with our shit. Because honest beats pretty every day of the week.

RESETTING HOW YOU DEAL WITH YOUR SHIT

Hitting the Reset Button on Toxic Coping Strategies

It was the summer of 2015 and we were just shy of the one-year anniversary of our move to Florida. Things were better. I was making more money and getting to reach new professional heights, Greg was excited about starting his new mortgage business, we were both proud that he hadn't had a drink for nearly ten months, and I was one full month into my own sobriety. On the outside, all signs pointed to maintaining the status quo. Why mess with what was so clearly working? Instead, I decided to resign from my position at Discovery.

Crazy, right?

On the outside, it seemed nonsensical to quit my lucrative job. This incredible opportunity had basically fallen into my lap at just the right time. It was helping our family crawl out of our financial hole; it helped relieve Greg of financial pressure, so he could focus on building the relationships required to get his business off the ground; and he and I were both in a calmer place since we stopped drinking. Yet, I was contending with an increasingly louder voice in my gut telling me that my job was the opposite of what I needed. Much of the work I'd been doing on myself was learning how to place greater value on my inner guide rather than outside voices, so what should I do when it's telling me to leave this job that seems like it's exactly what I should be doing?

We all make assumptions about people from what we see on the outside, and this situation is a great example of why doing that is a waste of time. I knew this job was in the wrong place at the wrong time. Contrary to appearances, Greg and I were still trying to figure out what our new life looked like, and things were sometimes turbulent. All of that work I had done creating my priority pyramid was void if I kept working at Discovery. The job required me to travel a whole hell of a lot. Sure, I could say that my family was my top priority, but if I was never physically there for them, how could I stay true to that? Worse, my job was leading me straight into a Cameo danger zone. Although I felt confident in my sobriety, I knew that triggers were still out there. With all of the traveling, time in hotels, and sales dinners, there would be so many opportunities for me to fall off the wagon. As much work as I had done at that point, I was still fragile. I knew myself well enough to know that being away from my family, under quite a bit of stress, without alcohol as a crutch was too much for me. The role I played was big and important, flashy even, with lots of entertaining and time alone—meaning big highs and big lows. The allure of being swept away by the "importance" and attention this position offered was a threat to the person I wanted to become. It was the exact sort of job that my younger, lone wolf self would scream with delight about. But my more mature, focused, determined-to-not-fuck-my-life-up-again self knew it was lined with traps. There was simply too much room for transgressions. The more I thought about it, the more I knew my gut was right. No amount of money could replace the time I was missing with my family, the risk of falling off the wagon, the loneliness, and the alone time that could potentially lead me to seek out toxic, external attention. It was time I claim *extreme ownership* over my decisions.

"Extreme Ownership" is a philosophy I learned about and held on to after reading retired Navy SEAL officer Jocko Willink's book of the same name. I like to think of it as turning a laser pointer onto myself to determine my role and responsibility for whatever situation I find myself in. Forget scapegoating, forget what part others have played, and forget what family, friends, and even society think should or shouldn't happen. How did *I* contribute to the place I'm at and what steps do *I* choose to take next? In the case of my job with Discovery, taking extreme ownership meant not lying to myself about the threat that the role had on the life I wanted for myself and my family. It was giving myself agency to acknowledge that the risks were too high. I didn't lie or fool myself into thinking I could handle it or I could suck it up and manage. I knew who I was at that moment in time and, more importantly, I acknowledged my limits.

It would have been so easy to be swayed by what this job looked like on paper, to be convinced by the whole "should" factor. But I was no longer living a life of "should," nor was I worried about what anyone else thought was right or wrong. I knew leaving Discovery was what I needed. No matter how much it sucked. No matter how crazy, even when—*especially when*—it didn't make sense. I was giving credence to my inner guide. We all have one. And this is one of the first times I truly went against the grain and listened to it.

Greg wasn't so excited about my new revelation. He understood my reasoning, but there was definitely a part of him that wished I could just stick it out for another year, just until his business was off the ground and our head was above water. In other words, a part of him wanted me to sacrifice my comfort and step up to the plate to save us. In fairness to him, his business was only six months old. He was bringing in very little income even though he was working his ass off. In his mind, here I was piling more stress and pressure on him by suggesting I quit my steady, reliable gig. It's easy to see how my idea could be met with some contempt. He felt like everything was being put back on his shoulders (all while he was still healing his broken heart and spirit).

It would have been so easy for us to draw the battle lines here. I wanted to quit my job for me and my family. He wanted me to stick it out for a year for him and our family. The ingredients for arguments, resentment, and miscommunication were all there. And in the old days, we would've screamed about it, drawn metaphorical blood, and then partied and drank ourselves into a state of not giving a shit anymore. But we weren't that couple any longer. Knowing that we didn't have the cushion of getting plastered after a balls-to-the-wall fight made the argument somewhat less desirable. And, without the alcohol, we lost the chance to numb ourselves of our anger, resentment, and really any feelings at all. So we were stuck having to contend with our feelings whether we wanted to or not. Thankfully, pairing our sobriety with the work we did on our partnership allowed us to not only be more comfortable with uncomfortable feelings, it also meant that we both tried to respect the other person's position. Alongside Greg's contempt was a desire to hear me out and understand my feelings. The same was true for me regarding him.

I should also mention that when I pitched leaving my job at Discovery, I also shared my desire to join Greg in his new business. I wanted to be partners. It felt only natural that if I was going to be earning commissions and establishing long-lasting business relationships that I should be doing it for our company. I was so confident that together the business would succeed because at the foundation of our new relationship was respect. We appreciated what the other brought to the table.

After his initial shock, Greg listened closely to my reasoning and soon agreed with my idea. We've been working together ever since.

I truly believe that none of these decisions would have happened the way they did (or at all) if I was still drinking. I would've enjoyed that liquored-up spotlight in a way that just doesn't serve me when I'm sober. And Greg wouldn't have shared his concerns about me quitting. Instead he would have just swallowed that contempt down with a case of beer. It's not that he and I don't fight or that there's never resentment or anger; it's that alcohol had become such a placeholder for everything we felt and should have expressed to one another but were too afraid, angry, or vulnerable to do so. In lieu of our toxic pastime, Greg and I each had to come up with our own "face-it" strategy. For me, I often lean on those "conversation trains" I mentioned in an earlier chapter. It helps me separate my true self from my ego by continually asking myself why. Here's an example of how that internal conversation would go: *I enjoy a glass of wine. Why? What makes it different from a glass of tea or ginger ale? What does it provide? Relief? Why? Does it help? Does it hurt? Why?* And so on... Conversation trains take you from one stop to the next until you've drilled down to the point where you're faced with your absolute truth.

Releasing myself from the grip of alcohol as well as the hold the "shoulds" had on me shifted everything. Once I officially joined Greg in our business, we realized that all we truly needed to operate our company was our cell phone and Wi-Fi. So we made another choice that went against the grain: We went on a spontaneous thirty-day road trip with the kids. We visited friends and family in Ohio and Indiana and then went on to Colorado. The trip was a kind of kickoff to our new way of living. And there were so many significant firsts: first family road trip adventure, first taste of the freedom of working remotely, first time hanging out with many of our friends since we moved, first time sharing that we weren't drinking, and the first time navigating the triggers of being back around all of those familiar people, places, and things (including the skeletons of our past). And we did it! It was not without some hiccups or losing-our-shit moments, but perfection is never the goal. Instead the focus was on being present, having more substantive conversations with friends and family, and enjoying being with our kids instead of watching them play with others.

Though we were still fresh on the alcohol-free train, the trip solidified that not only could we do it but that everything felt richer as a result. It was a major milestone for us. This trip would be one of many for our family. It fulfills my need for adventure without excluding the people I love most in the world.

After our road trip, Greg and I began implementing new habits to maximize our productivity and build a business presence. We also decided that I should see how bodybuilding could fit in our new life. With my coach *and* Greg's input, I picked a show that was a few months out and started training for my first (and only) competition as an IFBB Pro. Looking back, I know that the structure of training helped my commitment to sobriety tremendously. It removed even the possibility of drinking and it added new purpose to the focus on my health. Greg and I both followed the plan and worked out together. As a result, it was the most enjoyable and easiest prep I've ever done for a show. Even though I was the only one who actually competed, we treated it as a shared goal. There was no more animosity, resentment, or passive-aggressiveness like there had been when I competed previously. Instead we had a greater sense of clarity and calm because we were working together.

I like to think that in place of using alcohol to deal with my shit, I chose partnership. And it helped everything. Even my sex life. Each time I felt anxious about not being enough for Greg, I was forced to understand the feeling rather than drink until the sensation was gone. That led me to be more open to sharing my feelings with Greg. This critical information helped Greg be intimate in ways that were more specific to me, which only brought us closer. It all led to a feeling of being a team, to having a true partnership. It also reaffirmed that it was me that he wanted to be with. And that was sexy. It made our love life so much more enjoyable.

Dealing with my shit made me realize just how many experiences I had taken a back seat on. I was there, but not really as a participant. For example, back in Ohio, a beach day meant Greg and I sitting next to a cooler of beer while we watched our kids play in the water. In Florida, however, a beach day means we all swim together, play, laugh, and *participate* in the day. Our connection deepens with every everyday adventure. The same thing happened with watching football. In Ohio, football was a sacred weekend activity. Early in our relationship, Saturdays were basically Ohio State Day. We would either go out to tailgate (Greg's band would often play the biggest tailgate) or head to some party or host our own. Sometimes festivities started very early in the morning and lasted well into the evening. The kids would obviously be with grandparents so we could have the freedom to party. No matter how the game ended, we'd take off to a bar to either drink our sorrows away or celebrate the big win. Sundays were spent hungover watching NFL all day and usually drinking the "hair of the dog." After all, wasn't football synonymous with drinking beer? It was impossible to do one without the other, right?

As fall approached that year and the football season began, we couldn't help but try out our favorite Saturday pastime, just without the alcohol. Wow, was it different! We still enjoyed it, but without the haze of liquor, we actually paid full attention to the game, and it was a little underwhelming for us. Aside from the big plays, the majority of the game was kind of boring and so damn long—not to mention the insane number of beer and alcohol commercials. I never paid attention to that before. It was surreal watching the ads of these people drinking and having the time of their lives. They were never stumbling or puking, and they certainly were never hungover. For the first time, I had this realization of how in-your-face and glamorized alcohol is. I even noticed it being snuck into animated movies for some "relatable" adult humor. I couldn't believe it! But rather than making me feel like I was missing out on something, it initially enraged and disgusted me. While I'm used to it now, it still makes me feel sad. Experiencing these "normal" activities from a different perspective really opened my eyes to how prevalent and socially acceptable drinking really is.

One Sunday the Bengals (my team) and the Browns (Greg's team) were playing on some NFL channel we didn't get at home. So we put our team gear on and took the kids to Buffalo Wild Wings. The whole day still stands out to me because 1) The kids wouldn't have been with us in the old days. We would have used this opportunity as a date. 2) The first thing we would have ordered would have been big Brutus beers and shots. And 3) We would have gotten drunker than we planned and likely made the dangerous decision to drive home, and we definitely wouldn't have been as present with our kids that night, if at all that day. This time, however, the kids came with us. We explained the game to them, drank water, and went home after it was over. It was a beautiful moment that really had nothing to do with the game at all. The kids got to experience something we really enjoyed, but it didn't take over our entire weekend. It meant we had time to explore other things.

Once drinking was no longer the focal point, so many different activities popped up. More than that though, we could evaluate how we liked something based on our participation, rather than how loaded it allowed us to get. Alcohol had robbed us of our ability to choose and thrive.

Although getting sober was a positive experience, there were still hard days. And they would blindside me. I still had triggers. We still had stress. We were still unwinding our past and dealing with some of the unprocessed trauma from it. But as we continued living life, it became easier to assess the people, places, and things that we wanted to invite in. We changed our language and framed things differently. Like, instead of "I can't drink," we flipped it to "I don't drink." Even though I accepted that I truly was powerless over alcohol, changing my language made me feel empowered instead of powerless.

Socially, we started going out more and that was sometimes difficult because other people were involved. It was triggering in a couple of ways. It was still a conscious effort to decline alcohol, and Greg and I (but mostly Greg with me) were still learning to trust each other. We were hypersensitive to people's intentions and, early on, probably expected the worst. As time went on though, it became easier to handle it if people ordered drinks in front of us. Still, I couldn't help but notice that those evenings were often more superficial. Both Greg and I have found that our enjoyment stems from meaningful connections with friends, and it's probably not surprising to hear that those deeper connections often come with sobriety. Hiding behind a layer of liquor allows people to show up as someone they may not truly be. Without it, you get the opportunity to truly get to know a person.

Removing my "emergency exit" coping mechanism revealed that whether I considered alcohol to be a problem in my life or not, it was woven into every fabric of my being and holding me back from knowing myself and the people I love. My experience with alcohol translates to almost any form of escapism: shopping, gambling, porn, work, gossip, bodybuilding, playing in a band, etc. These activities all have upsides, and there is certainly nothing wrong with a guilty pleasure. However, when the balance shifts from once-in-a-while fun to becoming a coping mechanism or a distraction, that's when it's easy to lose your way. If you're willing to look at your behaviors objectively, like the *what* and *why* you do things when you need a break, then you can understand more clearly how those things fit into your life.

HIT THE RESET BUTTON ON HOW YOU DEAL WITH YOUR SHIT

During the Reflection

What is your coping mechanism?
What have you adopted as your escape from the hard things? I primarily used alcohol to avoid things that scared me. Things like investigating the root and reasons for my behavior or dealing with my insecurities or revealing my vulnerabilities or uncomfortable conversations. I drank to either make myself braver or numb out my feelings completely. Think about how you deal with the shit that makes you squirm. What's your go-to escape?

How does your method of choice make you feel?
We are hardwired to seek pleasure and avoid pain, so it's completely normal to justify and validate our methods of escapism. But, after the temporary ether of escapism wears off, what feelings are you left with? Guilt? Shame? Pressure? Compounded anxiety? How does it impact your mental health or self-esteem? Alcohol provided me relief for a brief period of time, but nothing was ever actually resolved. It allowed me to deny the reality of things. It prevented me from addressing my feelings honestly. At the end of the day, it wasn't solving any of my problems; it was either compounding them or creating new ones.

How is your coping mechanism impacting other areas of your life?
Aside from how your coping mechanism impacts your inner world, ask yourself how it impacts everything else in your life. Does it add more negatives or positives? How does it affect your

relationships? Your motivation? Remember, everything has a cost. Any activity, whether positive or negative, will deplete your time. When you factor your time in, ask yourself honestly whether it's still worth it. If you're busy hiding out in your escape hatch all the time, then there's little left for anything else. In my situation, alcohol was taking up a lot of space in my jar as sand. Each time I decided to neglect what really needed my attention, that created more sand. This left little room in the jar for my main rocks—my marriage, my kids, my own health—and absolutely no space for anything additional like personal development or goals.

What do you fear will happen if you eliminate your go-to crutch?

Fear is real. There's no denying that. An entire series of physiological responses are set off when we sense danger. It's what signals us to run or hide, to fight or fly away. And for this reason, it has been an important part of our survival. It protects us. We become so accustomed to avoiding what we fear that we fear what will happen if we don't!

What worries come up when you think about removing your escape response? Do you fear unearthing repressed memories or trauma? Do you fear being ostracized from your social circle? Do you fear that you will be incapable of addressing uncomfortable people or situations? Do you fear it will be too hard and you will fail?

Is your coping mechanism in alignment with the life you want to lead?

When you're doing something you've always done—drink, shop, gossip, etc.—it can be hard to imagine your life without it. Especially when it feels normal. Especially when it isn't even classified as a problem. But remember, you're not concerned with "should" or what others decide is a problem. Your concern is with yourself and your priorities. So instead of focusing on whether others might classify your coping mechanism as a problem, ask yourself if the best version of you would still rely on it. Consider what the best version of you looks like. Does it join a club or team to avoid being at home with your spouse? Does it buy things you don't need on credit cards to feel good enough or to keep up with the Joneses? Does it get plastered in order to play a role or to numb out your insecurities and vulnerabilities? If the answer is no, then maybe that coping mechanism doesn't align with who you want to be.

During the Reset

Find an alternative approach.
When that squirmy feeling arises and your initial reaction is to run away from the discomfort, pause. Sit with that squirmy feeling. Breathe. Lean in. Be curious. As I've mentioned before, you don't have to keep doing things the same way simply because you always have. It is possible to train yourself (and your brain) to address and inquire about your feelings. Even if it feels overwhelming at first, each moment that you choose to accept what you're feeling, to acknowledge that your instinct is to escape but that this time you're bravely exploring how to face it, you are transforming yourself. Find a "face-it" strategy that you can implement instead of escaping. It doesn't have to be a conversation train, but it should be something that helps you safely and calmly question things. Maybe you go for a walk or a run. Maybe you meditate. Maybe you even alternate and try different things depending on the situation or your mood!

Stop rationalizing the negative impact.
After the temporary relief of your habitual coping mechanism wears off and you're left with the guilt, shame, or emotional baggage that comes with avoidance—be honest with yourself about the collateral damage. Accepting these negative emotions because you think it's what your deserve or because you've convinced yourself it hurts less than facing your pain only exacerbates your long-term misery. Trust me; I had to learn this the hard way. It doesn't make anything better and only stifles your ability to truly heal.

Get your jar back out.
When we aren't clear about what our big rocks are, escapism creeps in and robs us of our true potential. Explore the root of why you do the things you do. If you are spending a lot of time on "X," then confront that with honesty. Once you understand the reason why it's stealing your time, you can slowly peel back the layers and eliminate those distractions. "X" may deserve a spot in the jar, but assessing whether and why it does can determine how much space it takes up. For example, if you find that the reason you do "X" is to avoid something that's innately hard for you, then it's important to know that and address it. Once you no longer need it as an avoidance tactic, then you might be able to create a healthier relationship with whatever your "X" is.

Think about potential gain instead of loss.
There is a flip side to every coin. If you continue to avoid change out of fear, you will never experience the fortune of bravery. We often think about quitting something as a negative, and when we operate from negativity or fear, then we dampen our will. However, quitting something in order to align ourselves with our potential and our goals can be life changing, as it was for me once I flipped "I can't drink" to "I don't drink." Remind

yourself that you're allowed to focus on the positive possibilities! How you frame your choices can affect the outcome.

Create a vision.
Align all of your actions with the vision you created of your best self. Redirect your actions away from that need to escape your circumstances. Instead, reroute yourself toward a more mature and positive strategy that gets you closer to your vision. The result allows you to not only work through those difficult emotions and situations with more confidence but will also create a wonderful ripple effect in other areas of your life. Your inner guide can help you here, the same way it did when I was deciding whether to quit my job at Discovery.

When I stopped drinking out of frustration and feelings of being stuck and chose to read and journal instead, I began resolving some of my negative feelings. New possibilities arose from that, which helped me take small steps toward the vision of myself I was striving for. Another ripple came from realizing that working at Discovery wasn't right for me. It caused me to partner with Greg, which then allowed us to go on a family vacation that would have been impossible had I not left my job.

During the Reinvention

Cultivate a newfound sense of empowerment and authenticity.
Choosing to embrace temporary discomfort takes you on a journey of courageous introspection. Confronting your toxic coping mechanisms is, at first, a more difficult path. But it's also more fruitful. It's empowering. Remember that as you try alternate strategies to face adversity, foster self-awareness, and, ultimately, transform your reality.

Going against the grain, while it at first can make you feel slightly uneasy, can ultimately feel incredibly freeing. When Greg and I decided to go road tripping with the kids only weeks after I left my lucrative job, we knew it looked "crazy." But our inner guide and our newfound logic ignored all of that. We empowered ourselves to know and act on what was best for our family.

Reclaim agency over your mental health and self-esteem.
When you alter your behavior and adjust what you'll accept for yourself, you undergo a profound shift in your emotional landscape. Confronting the true impact of your coping mechanism liberates you from the why-don't-I-ever-feel better cycle of temporary relief (that's so often followed by guilt, shame, and compounded anxiety). This newfound honesty with yourself leads to a sense of liberation and empowerment. Through this transformation, you cultivate resilience and a deeper understanding of yourself, paving the way for genuine healing and lasting growth.

Keep your house in order.
Living a life of extreme ownership creates a lot of clarity. I use this concept as a way to assess my side of the street in situations. I don't mean that I take blame for other people's behavior, rather that I own my part in it. For example, if Greg is upset about something and loses his shit, I rewind the tape in my head to see what my contribution was in escalating the situation. Then I ask myself what, if anything, I could learn and do differently. For me, extreme ownership does not mean that I am responsible for Greg losing his shit; that's for him to evaluate. What I try to do, however, is pull my piece of it out and analyze that.

When you know what is most meaningful to you and then make hard decisions about what's not, you know what people, places, and things to limit or eliminate. Often, this starts with external interests and moves to internal healing. This is a healthy cycle: eliminate the clutter, do a deep clean, then restore by adding back the things that bring you joy. For example, when I stopped going out with the sole mission of getting loaded, it made room for me to understand why I was making those choices in the first place. It also gave me the space to figure out what would be more fulfilling in the future. Had I not eliminated the drinking and partying piece, I wouldn't have had the time or ownership to do the deep inner cleaning that helped me redirect my focus. Ultimately, this effort, though challenging in the beginning, can create a life that is full of love and depth, hell yes!

Be fearless.
Physiologically we experience fear and excitement the same way. Our heart rate increases, adrenaline spikes, our minds begin to race, and our palms may get sweaty. By changing our dialogue from negative to positive, we train ourselves to feel a different way when we experience fear. With time and consistency, it becomes natural to see potential instead of deprivation. You build enough evidence to trust yourself so that even when something feels too hard or too scary, you can recognize the alternative to fear and move toward that instead.

Become your vision and share it!
There is nothing more profound than the realization that everything you think, feel, and do are aligned. It's full of duality. It's peaceful and exciting. It's empty and full. It's less and more. All at the same time. The hard work pays off and though you continue to face difficult things, you become better at dealing with them while exerting less effort. And then, something really beautiful happens. You share your time and your energy with people who feel genuine and authentic, because you've become those things yourself.

Lifting the veil of alcohol made everything clear. It forced me to be honest with myself about things I didn't want to face. Things I had intentionally kept "blurry" for the majority of my life because it was just easier. Some of those things were inconsequential, but most were life changing. Making difficult decisions such as whether someone or something fits into the vision we have for ourselves is hard. It takes honest examination. But ultimately, it makes us. Don't be surprised if the uncertainty feels scary at first. That's normal because it's new. At times it may even feel gut-wrenching, because looking at things with a truth lens requires us to accept things as they are, rather than as we wish them to be. There may be loss as a result, but at the end of the day, it's worth it. Peeling back the layers of your feelings, your vulnerabilities, and what it feels like to live, love, hurt, and heal is revelatory. It erases the need for an escape, because it arms you with the ability to find your way through things rather than a way out of them.

SECTION 4

The Reset Ripple Effect on Parenting and Career

INTRODUCTION

THE RESET RIPPLE EFFECT ON PARENTING AND CAREER
OR ALL YOU OTHERS

Initial Thoughts

A while back, Greg and I were attending the wedding of a childhood friend. Our families were pretty tight growing up, so while we hadn't kept in close contact in adulthood, our relationship was still deep enough for us to be invited to the nuptials. At the reception, we were seated at a table—table 14 if I'm remembering right—that was pretty far from the stars of the event: the bride and groom, the immediate family, and the bridal party. Greg and I didn't care; we were happy to be a part of the celebration from wherever, but the reason I'm giving you this background is because at the wedding, as we sat down and introduced ourselves to our tablemates, one of the women commented that we were at the AYO table: the All You Others. That phrase has stuck with me ever since. And I think it's the perfect explanation for this section, which touches on parenting and your career.

By no means am I suggesting that parenting is not important. In fact, I consider it the most important job I have. However, to be perfectly honest, I'm still figuring it all out. As I apply Reset Button strategies to how I parent, I learn and grow and work toward clawing my way out of the abyss of confusion that many of us feel as we guide our children toward adulthood. So I'm not quite ready to share my "expertise" on this subject. That said, I have noticed how some adjustments to my parenting style has benefited my relationship with my kids. So I can at least touch on ways to impart the Reset Button for a calmer, more fulfilling relationship with your children.

As for careers, it'll come as no surprise that I'm no expert on this. After all, I had no clue about what I wanted to do professionally. But again, I've made enough wrong turns and difficult decisions to give a 30,000-foot view of things I've learned. I'd like to share how Hitting the Reset Button allowed me to go from feeling completely lost and unfulfilled to building a successful company and a number of brands without burning out or ignoring the "living" part of my life.

Although I may still be figuring some things out as it pertains to my parenting style and my career, I am 100% sure that using this method on myself and my marriage created a positive stream that flooded into both of those areas of my life. That's the beauty of the Reset Ripple Effect and I can't wait for you to experience it yourself!

HITTING THE RESET BUTTON ON PARENTING

Because I Said So

This chapter could basically be one sentence: Parenting is fucking hard. The end. Seriously though, if you care even the least bit about your effect on your children, hell, even if you simply have a pulse, parenting is quite possibly the hardest thing you'll ever do. But why? Why hasn't someone figured this whole parenting thing out yet? That's a question I've been ruminating on a lot lately. I guess for me, the answer is a simple one: There are infinite questions without any real answers.

Parenting feels like a maze with multiple paths, dead ends, twists and turns that confuse and challenge every aspect of your being. This maze also has random "hazards" in varying degrees of difficulty that pop up to further test your limits. Picture the obstacle course show *Wipeout* and you can visualize my meaning. You're not just navigating things during every waking hour; it often follows you into your subconscious, causing you to toss and turn and jolt awake from sweaty *Wipeout*-style nightmares. I'm finding out now that this maze of confusion doesn't end with your child turning eighteen either; the "finish line" or completion of the obstacle course is elusive.

When it comes to both your responsibilities and your emotions, parenting is full of the most extreme dualities. Navigating them requires the agility to change faster than you can blink. Affection AND discipline. Excitement AND sadness. Protection AND nurturing independence. Fun AND frustration. Confidence AND worry. The list goes on and on forever. The truth is, I still have no clue what I'm doing. And as someone who has spent the better part of their life furiously trying to become The Best at whatever I chose to pursue, not knowing how I "rate" as a mom is really difficult. Where are the Official Mom Awards? Where are the trophies and the gold stars? The old me would have longed for that kind of outside recognition and commendation. Some formal acknowledgement that I was doing it "right." When you're a parent, it seems like the only time you get noticed is when you're screwing up.

When Faith was a baby, someone once warned me that as soon as I felt like I'd figured her out, she'd change. That was proven true in her infancy and continued on through the toddler stage, the preschool and preteen years, and has been the case as she skedaddles into early adulthood. The same for Ben. The same for kids everywhere. You know what constant change doesn't align with, though? The need to control things. Early on, I felt like I had to control everything. Rightfully so. There's so much pressure to keep everyone alive. For someone like me who was so independent, the idea of being responsible for someone else's survival made me feel like I had to make all of the decisions. Honestly, I think that's pretty understandable when the kids are babies, because they depend on you to do everything for them. This was especially true with Ben because of his birth and hospital experience. As they started becoming their own little humans, however, I struggled with letting go of the steering wheel.

I wouldn't say I was an overly rigid drill sergeant or helicopter mom when they were little though. I was actually pretty fun! We did lots of active things and often my primary role was taking my kids, along with other friends' children, to playgrounds, water parks, and other fun, adventurous places. We played a ton. But instead of really getting on their level and creating space for them to have input, I was usually the one making the choices of when, where, and whether I felt like it. It was a whole Boss vibe. Instead of recognizing that part of their development meant allowing them to make certain decisions and then realizing the reward or consequences of them, I would sternly communicate that things be done the "right way" (i.e.: my way).

Taking control and being authoritative can seem like the right way to parent because if kids know they have no decision-making power, it's easy to assume you'll avoid conflict. Yet, the opposite was often true. I was actually creating it. When Faith wouldn't clean her room my way, I would explode in frustration and she would feel inadequate, challenged, and frustrated. Ben, my rambunctious, messy, loud kid, was someone I'd instinctively feel the need to contain. As if his infectious energy and expressiveness was somehow inappropriate. My intentions with both kids was to steer them in the right direction. Kids need to learn how to clean their room properly. They also need to learn how to behave in certain situations. Right? In the early days, I ignored why I felt so shitty or inadequate when I expressed (i.e.: yelled) my rules and expectations to them, telling myself I was experiencing the normal feelings of defeat around parenting. I assumed it was what it was and that everyone felt defeated by or confused about the whole parenting gig sometimes. Waving my feelings away like this allowed me to just keep moving forward without ever really analyzing why I was so edgy about it all.

Then our lives blew up. We moved. We changed everything. And I went inward.

As Greg and I hit the Reset Button and renovated our lives, the work that I did to understand my childhood, behaviors, and

The Reset Button

decisions all played into the changes that I made as a mom. In some areas, I've nailed it. In others, I get it right sometimes. But I still miss. Over and over again. The difference, though, is my awareness. Before all of this work, I had no idea or even true interest in why I did or said the things I did.

The ripple effect of the Reset Button is that once you give yourself permission to be brutally honest and vulnerable in one area of your life, it naturally dominoes into other areas. My "right way" to parent doesn't seem so obvious anymore. Resentment and defeat isn't just accepted. Those feelings get filtered through this work, which ultimately leads to less explosive, more thoughtful parenting.

Over time, my mom rigidity has become much more malleable. To this day, I know what I believe a clean room looks like. However, if Faith's version doesn't completely align with my own but is age appropriate or a form of expression for her, then frankly: what the hell is my problem? Ben is a thoughtful kid whose energy and enthusiasm I actually admire, so why am I sending him the message that he is too much? Look, sometimes I still forget. Sometimes I can feel myself reacting, but then I remind myself to remember what it feels like to go into the gauntlet of middle school every day or to miss my boyfriend who is away at college. Taking that moment to shift my focus also serves to calm me down and remember that these two humans are the biggest rocks in my priority jar.

There's so much vulnerability in parenting too. Sometimes I'd think: *I have to be vulnerable again?* But I've found that embracing it has really helped. As time has gone on, I've become comfortable even sharing my insecurities around parenting with my kids. Expressing that I've never been a mom of teens before and honestly asking them to have patience with me too as I figure it out has given them the chance to exercise their empathy and invites them to see things from a different perspective. If I just bulldozed into decisions and pretended that I knew best all of the time, it not only would have stunted potential conversations, it also wouldn't have given them the opportunity to become more socially and emotionally mature. I know this to be true, because I see it every time I slip back into old behaviors and reactions.

As I've developed my approach to motherhood, I try to keep better track of my own behavior. By applying what I've learned about Resetting Myself, I'm able to more handily focus on the aspects of the relationship that I can control, as well as ensuring I'm keeping my side of the street clean.

Keeping my side of the street clean as it pertains to parenting has seemingly boiled down to compassion and communication. No matter the emotion, the obstacle, the age, etc., I've found that if I try to understand their perspective and communicate effectively with my kids, we stay connected. Does that mean it always happens? Hell. No. It's a constant battle to remember what it felt like to be where they are. It's an even larger battle not to project my judgment about what to do or not do based on my own collection of examples, experiences, and expectations. Trying to lead and follow at the same time (yet another duality) can feel impossible, but I keep at it, because when it works, it really, really works!

Then there are those days when I've just had enough. As Faith got older, she naturally began pushing back on me sometimes. And whoa, did I need to check my instinct to go all "my way or the highway" on her. I have to fight that desire to win. But I'm not perfect. Sometimes my mamma bully still rears its ugly head. When it does, I do my best to own it. To show her that I'm human; I too can push boundaries too far. I want her to see that when I am too controlling or dictatorial, I take responsibility and apologize for it. My hope is that she learns that apologizing isn't weakness and pride shouldn't always win the day.

Different kids bring on different challenges, too. With Ben,

The Reset Button

there hasn't been as much pushback, but there have been instances where he's gotten into minor trouble at school. So while he doesn't trigger the same buttons in me as Faith does, he does gear me up for overreacting when he does something "wrong." In my youth, even though I could be wild behind my parents' backs, I presented as a good girl, a rule follower. I rarely got into trouble, so I'm prone to overreacting when Ben has been called out for whatever infraction. But again, my reaction is about me, not him. So when I jump to conclusions or don't allow him to explain the situation before I launch into reprimand, I'm acting from my childhood, not his.

These days, when I'm triggered as a mom, I've developed the ability to know what tools to use to uncover and address the real issue. Often it's that I'm feeling unheard and/or exhausted. I mean, how many times can you say something before you lose your shit? We are human after all. It's frustrating and draining. When I do lose it, it's usually because my feelings are hurt or I'm running on empty and have nothing in the reserves to give. It's rarely truly about my kids' behavior and more likely that I'm hitting a stumbling block within myself.

Over time, Greg and I have come up with some mental guidelines regarding parenting. We believe that instead of demanding respect, we first have to give it. Kids need to feel heard in a way that makes sense to them—to both learn how to hear someone out and also how to respect someone. For example, if I expect them to respect my space and things, I need to respect theirs—even when I may not agree with how they maintain their space. I also need to inspire curiosity by showcasing and explaining why things are important, to all of us, so they can garner a full understanding of it, rather than just insisting on it "because I said so." Trust also falls under this category. As the kids have grown up, we've learned together that when trust is reciprocal our kids don't feel the need to hide things. Further, when they understand that punishment is not first and foremost on our mind, they're more likely to let us in. We reward that by navigating whatever issue with empathy and forgiveness. It doesn't mean there aren't consequences; it means that the learning and listening part comes first.

Here's the truth though: One second, I'm nailing it. I'm ready to walk onstage to accept my Best Mom award. The next, I'm blindsided by a new challenge—from an accident that requires stitches, a call from the school principal, hormonal mood swings, arguments with friends, or a breakup—and I feel like I'm back to square one. But I always have the Reset Button strategies to help me find my way again. I challenge myself to cede control and take it all step by freaking step. By taking the focus off of me and how I'm feeling, I'm able to more readily assess how my kids are doing and how they're understanding the situation they're in. It requires agility that even professional athletes might shy away from. But in the end, I believe that if I do my job mostly well, I'm helping to give my kids the tools available to them when life gets challenging, and hopefully that perseverance sticks.

If the Reset Button is an antidote to the "shoulds," then it's also an antidote to looking outward for mom recognition. Any parent trying to do their best can't help but internalize society's messaging that to get it "right," you have to have it all together—from prepped snacks to holiday goodies to bring to school to kids who make the honor roll and never get in trouble. And this is all while your house stays clean, the milk never goes bad, the laundry is always done, and a home-cooked meal is ready at 6 PM. I don't know about you, but my life sure as hell doesn't look that way. These days, if (really, when) I find myself throwing a snack to my kids as we run late to some after-school activity, I'm well aware that I'm not meeting the outside expectations of doing it "right." But once I got rid of the parenting "shoulds," I realized that I also got to redefine what doing it "right" meant to me.

I believe that being a good mom (notice I didn't say perfect) means learning how to pivot. Learning how to accept others' emotions and desires, their interests and identity. After all, perfection is subjective and not everyone's strengths fit into society's good parenting mold. In lieu of the hamster wheel of doing it all and then wallowing in resentment when I inevitably fail, I've tried to focus on creating a space where my kids feel safe and free to become who they want to be. Providing this room has opened the door to me learning from them too, which is incredible.

Here are some ways Hitting the Reset Button has helped me when it comes to parenting. Like I said, I'm still learning, but there's no denying that my relationship with my children and my satisfaction with my "job" as their mom has gotten so much better.

HIT THE RESET BUTTON ON PARENTING

During the Reflection

Are you getting on their level or are you expecting your kids to come to yours?
Did it sound familiar when I shared that I was a fun mom—as long as it was always on my terms? Each new age and phase has reshaped what this looks like, and while it has seemed easier, more efficient, more "appropriate" for me to make the choices, I've learned my idea of fun tends to be more complicated, elaborate, or intense than what the kids actually want and need. (Think over-the-top birthday celebrations, when all the kids really want is to play and have cake and ice cream!) Simply asking for and accepting their input has proven time and time again to be a more fulfilling and memorable experience for all of us. How often do you choose activities that your child enjoys versus activities that you prefer? Can you find balance between the two?

Are you approaching parenting from a "My Way or the Highway" perspective?
"Why?" Every kid's favorite question. We want them to be curious, right? What happens when we don't have a great answer? When the only words I can utter in response are "Because I said so!" then I've learned I have to step back from boss mode and step in as a team player. There isn't one right way to do any one thing. If I want my kids to be curious and open to new ideas, I have to consider that demanding they do things my way "because I said so" stifles their ability to learn and shape their own view of the world. Think about how much conflict, frustration, "shoulds," and shame are imposed onto them when we're stubborn and closed off.

Are you communicating your needs to help them understand where you're coming from?

As parents, we often ask our kids to share their feelings, so why does it feel wrong when we do the same? Understandably, we don't want our kids to feel responsible for us, but expressing our needs when appropriate models vulnerability and teaches compassion. It reminds them that we, too, are human. I realized I was withholding my feelings to protect them, but from what? I was never making them responsible for me. And showcasing my own vulnerability empowered them to express their needs without shame. Do you find yourself holding back your feelings and concerns, leaving you feeling frustrated and unheard? Are you projecting your role as the fixer onto them out of fear of being too burdensome?

Are you listening to their needs and helping them learn through true curiosity?

Look, no matter how hard you squeeze and grip, kids are still going to have moments of defiance, they're going to make mistakes, they're going to be dramatic about things, and they're going to do things that make you shake your head and wonder what the hell they were thinking. But that's their job. Figuring out how to navigate and communicate how they can learn from their actions and choices is the best way to ensure they grow. I've had to ask myself a million times, am I creating an environment where they feel safe to express themselves and explore their interests? Am I asking open-ended questions, guiding them through problem-solving, and showing interest in their perspective? On the flip side, do they fear my over reactivity and authoritative response?

How often do you take the time to truly listen to your child's needs without jumping to your own conclusions? How can you encourage their curiosity in a way that supports their growth and learning?

Are you holding space for empathy, gratitude, and togetherness?
When I feel Bully Mamma erupting, I try to stop and take a few breaths and remember my gratitude for being their mom. When the negative language around parenting surfaces, I dig deep and flip it to "I get to," because it's true. When you're feeling overwhelmed, overworked, underappreciated, or just completely at a loss as to how to handle whatever you're facing, ask yourself: How am I showing up in this moment? Am I being the support I needed when I was in their shoes? Am I holding too many expectations for what "should" be happening or how they "should" be behaving? I'm not suggesting to be permissive around your kids being disrespectful or that you allow yourself to be walked on, rather, I'm encouraging you to pick your battles and stay present, because these temporary moments are important.

During the Reset

Join them in their world.
Allow yourself to forget about money, time, appearances, and practicality sometimes. Sounds nutzo, right?! Those things are driving forces for adults but not for kids. Our kids are in the moment and things that may seem trivial or wasteful to us can be crazy important to them and their confidence in their own decision-making. See the world through their eyes. Try spending the extra five minutes at the park or getting the ice cream cone. Next level it and play on the playground equipment or indulge in your own cone with sprinkles and eyeballs! Let them choose the activity of the day, even when it feels like a "less than" experience to you. These moments create space and memories. They create connection. Most importantly, by not making all of the choices for them, the kids are free to express themselves and form their own preferences.

Collaborate on the rules of engagement.
Rules and boundaries are an important part of life, especially when parenting. However, understanding why there are rules in the first place is just as, if not more, important than having them. That's not just for the kids but for us as parents too. Ditch the notion that parents know best. News flash: We don't! By being flexible in our approach to establishing and enforcing rules, our kids have the potential to not only innovate and grow but to also develop a sense of responsibility and respect for authority. Involving them in creating the consequences of broken rules helps them form their decisions and own their choices. Working together helps eliminate confusion and fear and establishes reciprocated trust and respect for each other.

When it comes to establishing rules or dealing with issues that arise, Greg and I often rely on the family meeting approach. It sets a collaborative tone for whatever we want to discuss and keeps anyone from feeling attacked or defensive. Greg and I might lead the meeting, but we don't "run" the meeting. Everyone has an opportunity to offer their point of view so we can all walk away feeling heard. It doesn't mean that we won't disagree, but it's a much more open style of communication. This also gives Greg and me the opportunity to be really clear about what our concerns are, whether that's by bringing up stories from our own past or by relating stories we've heard from friends. It has also helped me realize how much my kids understand. Sometimes I forget how complicated the world they live in is and how that's enabled them to think on a more complex level. Shifting our approach this way gives us all a chance to get to know each other better.

Show them you're human.
The pressure to have all of the answers and get everything right is immense. We want to be our kids' superheroes. Unbreakable.

However, we are creating a false narrative for them by acting as if we do not make mistakes or have needs and feelings. We are also potentially inflicting a ton of stress on them by expecting they know what we need and then being upset when they don't deliver. Take the pressure off of everyone by creating an open and honest space where you can communicate your needs with reciprocated respect and confidence. If you feel worried or intimidated by something, share that with them in a way they can understand. If you want them to consider your lens of experience (aka mistakes) as they make their choices, choose to have a conversation (notice I didn't say lecture). Apologize when you lose your shit. Show that you too have transgressions and help them understand that it's a superpower to communicate your emotions.

Let them try things and, for God's sake, just listen.
Look around. There are tons of parents living vicariously through their children. Greg and I also fell into this trap! Before the move to Florida, I wanted so badly for Faith to love softball and cheerleading, just like Mom. I also '"encouraged"' Ben from a very young age to "pick up the drumsticks," just like Dad. I'm sure you know where all this "encouragement" led—to the dark abyss of disappointment, feelings of inadequacy, resentment, and limitation.

When we moved to Florida, we took a different approach. We let the kids lead when it came to their interests. Even when we couldn't relate at all to what they got into! The only condition we had was that they finish what they started. That has allowed them to really do and become who they want to be, without the pressure of living up to our expectations or wasting time doing something they didn't enjoy.

The same philosophy came to their feelings. I thought it was my job to always have a solution, to give tough love and raise resilient and strong humans. But after the work I've done, I realize that it isn't always about that... they don't always want an answer. They don't want practical. They don't want to be judged. They want to be seen. They want a hug. They just want someone to listen. They want to feel safe. The world is harsh enough. By understanding their needs and encouraging them to explore the world and their interests themselves, you can find balance in preparing them for adulthood while nurturing the kid they are in the moment.

Wash your windows.
There's this story making the rounds on the internet called "The Dirty Laundry Story." It caught my eye because I think it made a great point about perspective. A woman was constantly complaining to her husband about the neighbors hanging their dirty laundry on the line to dry. Day after day she would look out the window and scoff, "Why do they keep hanging the dirty laundry up?" One day, she glanced out and noticed that the clothes hanging on the line were clean. "Honey, they finally got it! They hung clean clothes on the line!" To which he replied, "Actually, I just washed our windows."

Resetting isn't about ignoring problems or dismissing your feelings but about consciously choosing a different lens through which to view them. When I catch myself projecting my expectations onto my kids (looking out a dirty window), I try to remember that it is a privilege to guide and nurture them. When I view obstacles as opportunities, there is a shift in the entire vibe of our household. After experiencing the early medical traumas with Ben, I know all too well how easily I could have lost him. Sometimes it felt like a roll of the dice. Now that she is eighteen, Faith could begin pulling away from us, eager to start her own life. It feels like it could all go away in a blink. Reminding myself of this, even in the most challenging moments, helps create a supportive, loving space where everyone can thrive.

During the Reinvention

Develop an "if not now, then when?" approach.
Time with our kids is not something we will get back. It's hard to imagine when they are little, but as they get older, you begin to realize that you only have "x" number of summers left or "x" number of holiday breaks. The memories you create will someday be all that you have left. From things like being at their sporting practices to jumping in waterfalls to singing at the top of your lungs on a road trip to hugging them when they're scared of the dark... experience life together! Even when it's inconvenient. Even when you're tired. Even when it feels like it's not the best use of your time. Even when you're not interested in watching *Hannah Montana* for the third time in a row.

Challenge the "no" or "not now" response in your brain and consider a "yes." Sometimes it's as simple as letting them pick spaghetti for breakfast. Remember that ice cream and extra five minutes at the park? It may not have been how you saw the plan for the day going, but if not now, then when? These are moments they'll cherish; they'll become memories that will stick out in their mind and stay with them. It will stay with you too.

Encourage honesty, understanding, and accountability.
Establishing rules and consequences collaboratively has encouraged ongoing open communication. From early on, we emphasized that being honest is always the best policy, even if it is about something uncomfortable or troublesome. Though it has proven to be a delicate dance, by being consistent with this principle, it has helped them realize they don't have to hide things to avoid trouble. There will be consequences to their choices, and we certainly won't always like what they are telling us, but the consequences will be less severe because there was honesty and ownership from the jump. Have they still hidden things or

lied? Of course. But, by adjusting our parenting philosophy to accept that they are going to make mistakes, squirm, and try to hide things, we've established that it is our job to help them understand rather than make it worse or promote a closed-off, rebellious environment. We both experienced not being able to talk through things with our parents (not their fault, it just didn't always feel available), and so we learned things the hard way, the wrong way, got lots of misinformation from our peers, and allowed that to shape our self-worth and our decisions as teens. Trying to help them feel empowered in their decision-making has helped them know who they are and what they stand for first. It has cultivated a sense of trust and responsibility and helped them develop confidence in their moral compass. We've seen it firsthand as they've gotten older and faced adversity.

Lead by example, of what to do AND what not to do!
I have had no hesitation in showing my kids how to be brave, adventurous, bold, hardworking, and how to win or be successful. But I honestly think that they have learned more from me in the moments when I was scared, remorseful, disappointed, or failing. They've seen me work through those moments and try again. They've seen that even parents get it wrong. That even parents have consequences. That even parents have to say they are sorry. After spending years trying to show only strength and perfection, I finally set my ego to the side and took a big gulp of pride, allowing them to fully understand that I am just a flawed person also trying to figure it all out. In a sense, it gave them permission to be flawed too. By being open with them about things like ditching alcohol, our own teenage struggles, and our need for individual and couples therapy, it has helped prepare them for times where they might also need to shift gears and ask for help when something isn't working. Don't be afraid to

let your kids see you. You are a part of them and in doing so, you help them understand themselves.

Praise the effort, not the result.
Kids are trying to navigate so much as they grow and develop into their own person. Between school, lockdown drills, the needs of teachers, coaches, and parents, their own social growth, and, of course, social media, we can't possibly expect them to get it "right" all the time. It's just pressure, on top of pressure, on top of more pressure. Do your best to instill a healthy narrative about process over results so they can enjoy the experience rather than fret about the finish.

I haven't always been great at remembering that my kids doing their best might not match what I want their best to be. I once ran a 5K race with Faith where she spent the run stopping, whining, and proclaiming that she just couldn't do it. And while I encouraged her, I also made my disappointment clear. I was hard on her for not grinding it out. I also remember a vacation where I was upset with her because she wouldn't go snorkeling. In my mind she was being so dramatic. Why couldn't she just jump right into the water?! In both cases I didn't consider that her feelings were real. Maybe she did need to take breaks and walk some of the 5K. Maybe her fear of the deep ocean was genuine. With Ben, I've bulldozed over some of his social anxiety, his insecurities about his glasses, and the limitations his high-risk vision has imposed on him. I've channeled my inner learned behavior to forge through, instead of stepping back to help nurture his confidence.

By praising and rewarding their effort instead of their results with grades, emotions, and personal pursuits, they can find their own groove. And through this, they develop self-worth, confidence in who they are, and learn what it means to feel fulfilled.

Transform future family dynamics.
When you view your parent-child relationship through a clean window of empathy, gratitude, and togetherness, you're not only reinventing your own family's dynamics, you're also modeling these behaviors for when they become parents themselves, thereby replacing any toxic or unhealthy cycles from the past.

As our kids eventually set off to tackle their own *Wipeout* courses in life, we can only hope that we've let them enjoy being kids, not screwed them up too much, and equipped them with the tools to navigate their own obstacles with fewer bumps and bruises. But the most important thing I'd like to leave you with is the belief that it's never too late. Take it from me. Even if your children have children of their own, you can still make adjustments to your relationship through the lens of the Reset Button.

HITTING THE RESET BUTTON ON YOUR CAREER

Working It Out

When we're kids, everyone always asks what we want to *be* when we grow up. It's never what do you want to do or what careers/jobs interest you? It's more about how you want to identify *what* you'll be, not *who*. I became an expert in switching identities in my adult life. Each had its own column, its own personality, its own vision. That got me into a pool of confusion, dissatisfaction, and resentment. After bottoming out, I've realized we're asking kids (and ourselves) the wrong question.

As a kid, I wanted to be a pop star like Debbie Gibson (the Taylor Swift of my day). After all, I was a pretty serious musician and performing artist growing up. Yet, when I told people, they chuckled and symbolically patted me on the head, letting me know dreams like that were more fantastical than possible. I internalized that message and reset my expectations. In the back of my mind, though, I still longed for it—longed for that *something* out there that broke the mold I saw around me.

It's also worth asking what "I want to *be* a star" means in a broader context. What is that goal's essence, beyond the music? To me, it means being in a position of authority. Being admired for talent *and* for hard work. It means taking big risks for big rewards. It means having no limits placed on you. And finally, it means challenging yourself to be at the top of your game.

In a nutshell, that's really what I wanted. (Though I still never turn away from a microphone when it's in front of me!)

Other than when I stayed home with my kids, I've always worked. I came of employment age around the same time my parents were divorcing, so they had little "walking around money" to give me. I had to earn it. Over the years, I worked at a boat dock gas station, I bussed and waitressed, and I worked in administrative positions. The only one that gave me an inkling of satisfaction was the waitressing job, because I knew I had some control over how much I would make. The friendlier and the more on top of my game I was, the more I'd get tipped. I loved that potential. But it was still shift work that, even when I was tipped well, wasn't going to change my economic life. More than that, I dreamed of bigger things.

Few people in my orbit did something nontraditional with their lives. That's not a judgment on them. I just didn't have many models to look toward as an example of what "could be" instead of what "should be." But I longed for that "could be" career. Nine to five, salaried work always made me feel trapped. I'd watch the clock tick slowly by. My only outlet was heavy drinking and extracurricular drug use so I could completely zone out.

I spent a lot time trying to fit into the traditional life I saw all around me. It was like putting on a pair of jeans that are your regular size but still don't look or feel right when they're on. That discomfort with the "normal" path led me to take college courses early, leave college before graduating, and even secretly pursue an accounting job in New York City. Yet, every time I dipped my toes in any water that was unique to me, I would pull my foot back out again. Take the job in New York, for example. Eager to pave a new trail, I decided to follow my one friend who'd left Ohio to pursue modeling in the city. I found a listing for an accounting job and flew out there in secret—only telling about three people. I actually stayed there for several days alone, as my friend was out of town. I'll never forget getting dressed up in the power suit my mom lent me and walking to that interview. I will definitely also never forget nailing the interview and walking back out on the street afterwards. I was floating above everyone around me. I got the job! My life was (finally) about to begin. Part of what elated me was that I did it all on my own, with my own money, ambition, and vision. I had it all planned in my mind. I'd work there from nine to five, maybe wait tables at night, and also try out for musicals and other productions to pursue my performing arts dreams. I remained in New York for a few more days, taking in all that my soon-to-be-home offered. When I told my parents, they were definitely happy for me but also apprehensive. My mom could relate to my desire for "more," but she worried about me being so far away. My dad was concerned about me quitting college with no plan if the job didn't work out. Ultimately, though, they knew it was my choice and supported me. I was finally on the verge of forging my own unique path.

Back in Ohio a few days later, doubt crept in. How could I leave my friends and family? What if I failed and had to return home with my tail between my legs? I crumbled under the what-ifs. I ghosted the firm and stayed in Ohio. Bob and I got back together and I hoofed it over to a job placement agency (because I'd also ghosted the job I had in Ohio at the time, thinking I was moving to New York).

I was a college dropout who had to crash at my mom's apartment in Columbus. I wasn't directionless but I longed for something that I couldn't put my finger on. I eventually found myself working at the huge auto manufacturing plant in town. This was considered a big deal. Getting a job there, especially one in administration, was looked at as lucky. Yet I felt trapped and miserable. I was working seven to three, punching a time card, wearing a uniform, and being told where to be, when to be there, and what and how to do things. There was no room for my point of view, no sense of coloring outside of the lines, and it felt confining. There I was, twenty years old and feeling like a shell of myself. Honestly it was one of my darkest periods. I always partied, but I partied really hard during this time. And the one relief that I had was that I was able to pay my bills. But six months into the job, I was fired for being late too many times. This was my fifth job in two years that I'd either been fired from or just stopped showing up to.

While I was at the plant, Greg was back in Ohio also licking his wounds from his "failed" music career. He ended up sleeping on a mutual friend's couch in Columbus, which gave us a chance to reconnect. This was the time we were finally able to commit to one another. Both of us were eager to find a place in the world that suited our appetite for a full life. Together, we gave one another the confidence that maybe we didn't quite have on our own.

After I got fired from the auto plant, Greg encouraged me to connect with people I knew in the business world. Sure enough, a family friend offered me an opportunity at a large financial firm as a financial advisor. I was grateful because I might not otherwise have even gotten in the door since I didn't have a college degree. I was determined to prove myself and obtained three professional licenses in the field. Those countered my lack of a diploma with the career-specific credentials needed to be taken seriously. This role also taught me the importance of mentorship. The family friend's daughter was my coworker, but more than that, she was a great teacher. I finally had a job that could become a career. I was also in control of my schedule and was rewarded the better I did. I could determine how I made the sale and figure out my own way of doing things.

I'll admit, I didn't love cold-calling or walking into strangers' houses, but I did like helping people understand their financial picture better. It felt really good to guide clients toward meeting their goals and providing financial solutions. Mostly, though, I absolutely loved making the sale. I don't mean this in some kind of smarmy way. I wasn't into the hard sell. But I didn't fear rejection, was tenacious, and also had confidence in what I knew, so I was always sure that I could find something that fit my clients' needs. I felt more like a consultant than a salesperson and I really excelled.

Remember how I wanted to be a star? Although I didn't put it together, this job aligned with some of the aspects of what being a star entailed. I was earning people's respect and admiration, I was working hard at something I enjoyed, and it felt like there were no limits to what I could achieve. But again, I didn't quite put that together back then because on paper, pop star and financial advisor have nothing to do with one another, unless you count my killer karaoke skills at office happy hours.

Shortly before I started at the financial firm, Greg had transitioned to the mortgage business. We had simultaneously gone from feeling like the world had spit us out to feeling like we'd taken back control of our destiny. We were making money, falling in love, and enjoying every minute of our lives.

Remember that screeching record when I found out we were pregnant? Our life took a bit of a swerve. That swerve took my career with it.

When I was pregnant, going into strangers' homes felt increasingly uncomfortable, and so, along with my mentor, I moved to a different bank and got a more stable role as a banker. I was still selling (banking products now), though I was back in the realm of nine to five and the confines of the corporate world. But it felt like a better fit for the transition to motherhood. I quickly became a top producer because I worked hard to get to know my clients, building trust and a rapport with them. However, when I went back after my maternity leave, my feelings about the job got complicated. I missed Faith terribly, which was made worse by sitting in a cold employee restroom to pump breast milk throughout the day. By the time I got home, I was exhausted. As tired as I was, I hated that I only had a few hours with my baby, and I resented my mother-in-law for all the quality time she got with Faith while I was at work. I was also way too tired to deal with a husband who wanted to connect. It was a draining cycle. I was barely keeping all of the balls I was juggling in the air, constantly torn between work, family, and my own sanity. Things finally came to a head, and Greg and I made the decision that I would stay at home for a while. I was hugely grateful that that was even a possibility for us and so happy to have the time with Faith. Yet, the career-driven part of me felt abandoned. I couldn't win no matter what I chose. Ultimately, I was plagued with guilt and shame that I couldn't do it all.

I know many stay-at-home parents can relate to the confusion and sometimes lack of fulfillment that being at home all day with your child can bring. And that feeling is, of course, followed up with the guilt that you're not 100% all emotionally in on being there with your little one. I felt parenting Faith was my highest calling, but I'd be lying if there wasn't a part of me that was bitter that my career was the one that would take the hit. On top of *that*, I had to witness the beating our bank account took from losing my income. It was a lot of emotions swirling around and I shared none of them with Greg.

Soon into my time at home with Faith, Greg took the entrepreneurial leap into starting his own one-person branch with a new mortgage company. He excelled at mortgage sales and wanted to venture out on his own so he could control the entire process, as well as earn the entire commission. As Faith was aging into toddlerhood, I started helping Greg out more. I relished the opportunity. We knew that his timing for going out on his own made no sense on paper, but we didn't care because we felt like it was us getting back to our Cameo-and-Greg spin on taking the world by storm. So what if others thought we were reckless idiots? We were feeling that late teen/early twenties dreamer-energy and applying it to our grown-up lives. We colored outside the lines even further when Greg took two months off to tour with Leo (our favorite band). I knew I could cover for him at the company and there was no way he could miss out on the opportunity. When it was feasible, I flew out to join him, dancing in the crowd and living out a rock star wife's existence.

Not long after, it all imploded. The tour ended and the housing market crashed. We tried to keep the business afloat for too long and incurred a lot of debt. It felt like yet another failed attempt at blazing our own trail. So back to the corporate world we went. Faith was old enough for daycare, so I went back to being a banker.

Once again, I shot right up to being a top sales producer and was on track to becoming a financial advisor again. I was making more money and was nearly matching what Greg was earning. My managers became close girlfriends whom I respected both personally and professionally, and they empowered me to climb the ranks in this male-dominated field. Greg and I had debt to pay down and lessons to learn about when to pivot.

It took me about a year, but I was eventually promoted to a financial advisor position, giving me the freedom to make my own schedule, earn more money, reach a higher level, and have greater authority. Greg, too, was doing really well professionally. It was a great period of satisfaction for us. But we'd need to swerve and pivot once again because I was about to go into labor at twenty-four weeks.

We often look at our career as this monolith that stands separate from everything else. We're all scrambling to take care of our family and household while also advancing professionally, but we (and often our managers/bosses) don't integrate it into who we are as employees. Sure, we're given personal and sick days, and now there's the quippy work/life balance copy that companies publicize, but it's rarely applied in a truly organic way. That was my experience anyway. While I was helplessly watching Ben fight for his life, I was asked when I'd be returning to work. I'm sure you can understand when I tell you that work was the last thing on my mind! I understood my bosses had to manage coverage for me, but I couldn't keep myself from feeling judged. It was as if all the time I'd previously put in, all the hours I spent at work over being at home with my family, all of the mentorship I provided meant nothing. I'm also not immune to the comparisons that plague women about how they handle their work/life and career/motherhood balance. It all pissed me off. The truth was, even once we were sure Ben was going to survive, we were told his immune system would be very fragile. Daycare, and even babysitting by an extended family member, wasn't an option. So there we were, faced with another hurdle. My career abruptly halted. I'd finally felt I had truly hit my professional groove and then life hit us hard. I quit my job without hesitation, knowing I was doing the right thing for my son's health, but closing up that career door was sad for me. Greg was left to pay our bills and pay off our debt.

As Ben got better, my own resentment built. My loneliness grew. My anger toward Greg's lack of support accumulated as I got into bodybuilding and took on personal training clients. I confessed none of these feelings to him. Nor did he communicate his resentments to me. It was all just passive-aggressively brewing under the surface.

By the time Ben turned three, I had to go back to work. Our financial situation had grown dire. There were times we'd have to leave all of our groceries at the store because our credit card was declined. We needed to get serious about our financial health. Yet, I didn't want to return to the bank. I didn't want to leave Ben to someone else. Nor did I want to get back on that exhausting cycle of a forty-plus-hour workweek and then kids and a husband waiting for me and my attention at home. I didn't want to settle.

I needed someone to be mad at, so I was mad at Greg. I look at pictures during that time and you can see the rage in my face. Underneath, though, I was truly just sad. Sad that things weren't happening in the way I hoped. Sad that I didn't feel supported and that Greg and I weren't as connected anymore in our Big Goals. Instead, life was being dictated by the shoulds of the American suburban dream.

I eventually relicensed and went back to my financial advisor role, which didn't thrill me in the way it used to. My life changed and I changed with it. While I still did well, I didn't care. I was mad that I had to be there, in a subordinate role, and give up on my bodybuilding dream right after I went pro. I started drinking often and smoking again. And, as you know, I was having an affair. Soon after, Greg confronted me about cheating, and our marriage blew up and I imploded emotionally.

By the time we landed in Florida, our careers were pretty low on our list of priorities. Greg even took a little time off given the fragile state he was still in. Our debt didn't allow for both of us to ease into our new location, so I got right to work. I knew it was my turn to take on the financial pressure for the family and I did so willingly. It didn't stop me from being miserable though. I too was teetering emotionally, unsure if our marriage would survive, missing the security we had in Ohio, worried that this big gesture, this big move, was the wrong choice. I told myself this was temporary. And though I did well and worked hard, I knew I couldn't continue in the position long-term. I tried to work out at lunch, but there were also many days where I spent my break staring into the sparkling turquoise of the Gulf of Mexico while sobbing. That happened so often that I always made sure to have my makeup bag with me so I could freshen up before returning to work.

The Reset Button

Things got so bad that I started blowing off morning meetings (that I was supposed to be leading), cutting out as early as I could, and basically doing the absolute minimum. Six months in I went to Greg in tears and told him I just couldn't do it anymore. With the pressure of needing to make a certain amount of money and no professional experience outside of banking, I felt hopeless. I needed to do something, anything, to feel like I was at the very least taking steps to change my situation. I leveraged my status as a member of the International Federation of Bodybuilding and Fitness Professional League (IFBB) to seek out training and nutrition clients, timidly posting the announcement video on social media. I knew doing this wasn't a magic elixir that would change everything. At most it would start as a side hustle, but it aligned with something I loved. To my surprise, people responded right away. It was the glimmer of hope I was desperately looking for. That's when I got the call from an old friend about the job at Discovery. It was a godsend. It made me feel like I had value beyond banking. Within two weeks I was on a flight to Chicago to interview. I was prepared and confident (with my own power suit this time!) and had that same feeling leaving it that I'd had way back in New York City. I got the job and gave the bank my two weeks' notice.

Ultimately, the job at Discovery wasn't a fit for me for a multitude of reasons. But the opportunity saved me. I learned invaluable lessons—about my boundaries, abilities, professional strengths and weaknesses, and what's important for an overall high level of success. Although pivoting to working with Greg on his mortgage business is a completely different arena, I was able to take all that I'd learned at Discovery and apply it to my new role with him. Without that blip in my career history, I firmly believe I wouldn't be who I am today or operate at the level I do professionally.

Greg and I finally got to a place where our "should do" was completely taken over by our "could do." We wanted to be people who were in control of our own destinies, and that's what owning our own business does for us. And so neither of us are doing what we said we wanted to do professionally when we were kids—me a pop star, him a rocker—but we are living out many of the aspects of what having those careers entail. We make our own schedule. We delegate intelligently. We also have no limits. We take big risks for big rewards. We create our own vision of what our business looks like and can ensure it reflects our own values and principles. We've also learned to ask for help when we need it, especially in order to maintain healthy boundaries and avoid burnout. And here's the other kicker: Making music together is a priority for us now because we both love it. Not only that, but we recently started our own media company, applying everything we've learned in business and in partnership. So while we're not playing sold-out shows, we are jamming together, making albums, and having so much fun doing it. And that joy infects every other area of our life.

HIT THE RESET BUTTON ON YOUR CAREER

During the Reflection

What do you want to be when you grow up?
Think back to your original childhood answer to this question. Dissect what it was about that career, that label, that really interested you. Was it the actual role or was it the characteristics of what the role offered? How does your current career align with your childhood response of *what* you wanted to be? Is there overlap with the deeper essence of *who you wanted to become*?

Does your work complement your life or consume it?
How does your career integrate into the life you want to lead? Does it allow for you to spend time with loved ones? Does it give you the space to pursue other important goals? Do you feel your job dictates how you spend your time, how you view yourself, and how others perceive you? When someone asks you about YOU, do you find it hard to define yourself outside of your work? Are you invigorated or depleted by what you do?

What's in a paycheck?
Money is personal. The way we view money is often deeply ingrained in us from our early years. There's no denying we need it. That's a fact. Many of us also want more than we need for legitimate reasons like safety, recreation, and legacy. While choosing a career based on money doesn't always lead to happiness, not having enough of it can lead to increased stress. Finding the balance between income and peace is vital.

Get honest with yourself when answering questions related to money. Are your career decisions driven more by financial necessity or by personal fulfillment? Are you sacrificing your well-being for higher earnings? If so, is that okay with you? Is it okay with your family? Does your job provide financial stability or does it create stress and uncertainty? Does your income support the lifestyle you envision for yourself and your family? Or are you overindulging in lifestyle choices, perpetuating a cycle of constant catch-up? Do you feel limited in your choices because of money?

Do you feel pressure to keep all of the plates spinning?
Managing everything can feel suffocating. This is especially true when our career advancement depends on an unwavering commitment, even though we might already be spread too thin. Add to that a common, though unproductive, habit of comparing our spinning plates to others'. We make assumptions that everyone else has it all figured out and balanced, making us feel like "being enough" is available to others but elusive to us.

Are the expectations of your job reasonable? How flexible is your job in accommodating your personal needs and unexpected emergencies? Have you set boundaries between work and home life? Do you have support at home and ask for help when needed? How high is the stress of managing it all? What's being neglected? What long-term impacts might this have on your health, relationships, and career?

During the Reset

Find the connection in your career and yourself.
We can all get bogged down by what we do. Day-to-day responsibilities can rob us of the joy we felt when we first started a job. We lose sight of why we do what we do and how that fulfills us. This is an ongoing process of alignment and adaptation. We change. Our values may change as well. We may need to revisit

our priority pyramid, set new goals, take bold action, and be open to what "could" be instead of what "should" be.

Reclaim your time and identity.
Naturally, our careers can become a defining element of our identities because we spend so much time prioritizing them. The average forty-hour workweek eats up roughly 2,000 of the 8,700 hours we have each year. That excludes commuting, so it isn't even the whole picture of the amount of time spent away from loved ones or from pursuing other things for ourselves. Even if your career *is* your top priority, it doesn't have to define the entirety of who you are.

How are you spending your time? What are your boundaries? Separate yourself from your job by scheduling time for yourself and your relationships to ensure they don't get overshadowed. Rediscover the authentic "off-work" version of yourself and make sure people see that side of you too. Be open to exploring other opportunities. You may find greater peace by shifting your work so you have a shorter commute or discover that by lessening your workload you have more space to pursue other interests and avoid burnout.

Do what you love and money will often follow.
I think it's fair to say that different phases of life dictate what you need out of a job. Sometimes it's money. Sometimes it's growth opportunity. Sometimes it's fulfillment. I also think it's fair to say that it is possible to have all of what you need and desire at the same time. You don't have to sacrifice pursuing your dreams in the name of a bigger paycheck. I'm not saying throw caution (and your bills) to the wind, quit your job, and pursue your passion with no plan. What I am saying is that changing jobs should always be an option. The average person holds twelve jobs in their lifetime! Leading with what energizes you can open

you up to opportunities. It may not look like what you thought it would. It may not happen in the way you anticipated. It may be a transition in baby steps. Be agile and courageous as you look for ways to apply the essence of *who you are* to your free time or current moneymaking role.

Get rid of some plates, or at least set them down temporarily.
I don't know whether it was pride, stubbornness, or just the newness of it all, but the pressure to make my career and family life work cohesively together broke me. The constant grappling with how to manage the discordant priorities in my head proved impossible. Career desires would fight it out with home life, which was fighting how much attention to give my husband over my kids, and wait… what about my other interests!? I needed help, but I thought that made me weak. It was all a never-ending runaway train perpetuated by comparing myself to everyone else, to what society expected out of me, and to what I thought I "should" be able to do.

You'll always have more than one plate spinning. It's about knowing which ones need immediate attention and which ones can be set aside for a little while. Start by smashing the comparison plate! Then gauge which plates are no longer relevant in your life. You can always pick them back up when life changes. Of the plates that are left, are there any you can ask someone else to spin for you, even temporarily? Remember, the plates you are in charge of are the ones that correspond with your priority rocks.

Once you determine your boundaries, find a way to have open conversations with your employer, colleagues, friends, and family about them to ensure everyone understands and is prepared to respect them. Asserting your boundaries with others will also help you assert them with yourself and "be where your feet are." This proverb is all about bringing yourself back to the present whenever you're switching roles. For example, before you enter your home after work, take a few deep breaths, take your work hat off, and put the mom hat (or dad, or spouse, etc.) on. This not only centers your mind to where you are, it also mitigates feelings of overwhelm that come with doing it all.

During the Reinvention

Never work a day in your life.
Mark Twain said, "Find a job you enjoy doing, and you will never have to work a day in your life." I always thought that was bullshit. But as I've worked to create unity between my work and my purpose, I've discovered it is true. It can be for you too!

Identify the core elements that motivate you. Whether it's serving or making an impact on others, being an innovator and problem solver, or inspiring others through creativity, when your work aligns with what inspires you, it transforms your job from a checklist of to-dos into a pursuit that enhances your overall fulfillment.

You are more than your career.
Identifying closely with your career isn't a bad thing. It can be a source of pride, independence, and fulfillment. However, once you reclaim space in your mind and time in your schedule for other things to explore and pursue, your life will become richer. You'll connect with people who see you more deeply, and you'll develop a more well-rounded, resilient, and healthy sense of self.

You can be a billionaire!
While giving corporate keynotes, my friend and mentor Jesse Itzler has shared the story of how he encountered the acronym SIPPS (Social, Intellectual, Physical, Purposeful, and Spiritual).

In researching retirement communities for his parents, he observed that some of these facilities used SIPPS to assess incoming residents' well-being. Notice that financial isn't even a category. Jesse explains how we often neglect our values while we are busy growing our finances. He goes on to share that his father, Daniel Itzler, who ran a plumbing supply house, was never rich but was a "spiritual billionaire."

The message: Money isn't everything. "If you have a billion dollars and your spirit is zero, a billion times zero is zero."

I hadn't heard this story when I made the choice to leave my financial advisor job or when I left Discovery because I was away from my kids too much. But I like to believe that somehow I just knew. I didn't quiet that voice inside of me saying that I could have it all—that I didn't have to sacrifice my spirit. I allowed myself to believe it.

When you get clear on your own unique sense of harmony between money and passion, you can truly find cohesion for yourself.

Move with more fluidity and intention.

After doing this work, you should be spinning fewer plates. You're also rotating your remaining plates with less stress, guilt, and resentment—moving with more fluidity, lightness, and freedom from unnecessary pressure. Every plate matches up with your priorities. When those priorities change or you're thrown a curveball, you'll know how to figure out a way to reassess. Nothing gets overlooked or neglected. You can breathe. Most importantly, you know that your work and the people and things most important to you are getting the best of you, not just the rest of you.

SECTION 5

INTRODUCTION

MAINTENANCE

Initial Thoughts

I began writing this book over four years ago. Man, how time has flown! Since then, I've faced moments of self-doubt, setbacks, and times where I had to recommit myself to the tools and strategies I outlined in earlier sections. Life can be extremely challenging, juggling responsibilities, goals, and curveballs, so it's only natural to feel a pull toward all the chaos. It's in those moments when you need to take a step back and remember how to right yourself again. Maintenance is the work of creating a practice that sustains you through whatever is thrown your way. Since beginning this book, I also have developed some fresh perspectives to share on how to incorporate this practice into your everyday life.

As I said before, the Reset Button is not a one-time gimme. It's the alarm you push to stop yourself from repeating strategies you already know don't work, to think deeply and honestly about how you can right yourself again, and then to give yourself permission to actually do the things. Over and over again.

MAINTENANCE

Leaning on that Reset Button

Life is interesting, isn't it? Ever feel like once you finally figure out all of the answers, they (whoever "they" are) change the questions and back to the starting line you go? Me too. Who's in charge here? Oh wait... it's me. I am in charge of my life choices (notice I didn't say *in control of my circumstances*). And here's a little tough love for you: YOU are in charge of yours. My life changed drastically once I realized that if I wanted to achieve the results I desired; it would be up to me to start asking the questions. Each time I return to the starting line, I'm armed with more experience, more knowledge, and most importantly, an opportunity to continue the quest of living my most optimized life. That is the essence of the Reset Button. It's the empowerment to take charge. It's the permission and guidance to start small, to start again, to start from the beginning, to start where you are, hell, just to START... and refine the process as many times as you need to. And that's what this Maintenance chapter is all about.

Maintenance is a funny word, because we think of it as keeping the status quo—or maintaining whatever it is that we've worked toward. We lost the weight; then we maintain it. We trained to run a marathon; then we maintain that fitness level. The difference here is that where the Reset Button is concerned, you're not meant to stay in some kind of stasis. Instead you're meant to *stay* in an active, thoughtful state. You should be actively questioning, analyzing, ensuring that you are living your life according to your priority pyramid. The only thing that you are maintaining is an active Reset Button practice. I point this out because I don't want to give you a false sense of completion. Life is ever-evolving and so are you. The idea of completion runs counter to our own growth, our relationships, our career, and our place in the world.

When I'm asked, "How did you just pick up and move across the country?" or "How did you stop drinking for good?" my response is always the same. What helped me then, and what continues to help me now to overcome the fear associated with change, is the notion that I know what life looks like as it is. I know the results of the choices I've made or am making. If I make different choices and it yields undesirable results, I can always go back to what I was doing before. My hometown will always be there. The corporate job, or one like it, will always be there. The happy hours will always be there. And yes, the suffering relationships and patterns of dysfunction will likely always be there too, ready to bring me back into the fold. However, if I make different choices and it yields results that are favorable or even just slightly more in alignment with my goals, then it's a risk worth taking.

Author, entrepreneur, and speaker Marie Forleo says, "Everything is figureoutable." I love that. It means we can overcome any challenge when we are persistent and have the right mindset. Let's be honest, though, most of us are more willing to (begrudgingly) deal with circumstances when they're forced on us, rather than being proactive and making a new choice for ourselves. However, if we consciously choose to bet on ourselves, no matter the circumstances, and we challenge ourselves to stay open to figuring things out along the way, we're less likely to be forced into any one position. Approaching choices, decisions, and relationships this way can also be less scary.

There are many things I've done in my life that I'm not proud of. Things I've said. People I've hurt. Regretful choices I've made. Choices I *didn't* make. Many of them I've shared with you. Many times I've wished I could go back and change those things. Actually, what I really wish is that I'd had my Dorothy from the *Wizard of Oz* moment much sooner and realized that I had the power within me all along. That I could make the necessary changes that might have salvaged situations or kept them from happening in the first place. I wish I'd been more curious about my behavior and decisions with regard to my past and my future and then acted on that curiosity with courage and intentionality. I also wish that back then I'd had the power to forgive myself, and others, and be free to move forward without all that added weight of shame. Looking back, it's easy to see how utilizing the 3Rs of the Reset Button could have saved me from spinning out of control. How it could have provided me with more clarity and confidence. It would have enabled me to break free from the never-ending cycle of frustration and confusion around why I wasn't feeling fulfilled.

While I can't go back and "fix" any of the mistakes I've made, accepting and learning from them has been imperative to living a forward-facing life. Through my growth, I've learned that *making* mistakes is also essential to thriving. It's difficult because we can only see what's right in front of us. Often, we don't even realize we're making a mistake. What's more, sometimes they're not even *our* mistakes. It's also hard to fathom that errors in judgment or action can be the catalyst for change. That screwing up can lead to something better. And that sometimes the (often negatively perceived) existential crisis is just what we needed. Especially when we're deep in the pain. I was at a conference years ago, and one of the speakers (my apologies, as I can't remember their name) said, "If you can't find the gift in your pain, you are just left with pain." I think of this quote whenever I need a reminder to stay patient and optimistic during challenging times or uncertainty.

Fear of making a mistake can be a huge reason for why we fear change. You likely don't have to look too far to see someone around you staying miserable because it's comfortable. Maybe it's you! I personally dwelled there, frustrated and unaware, until our Rock Bottom moment completely obliterated the life I was living. In my mind, status quo was the way to go. Everything was *fine*. Instead of leaning into brutal honesty and accountability—*my marriage is suffering because I'm closed off and afraid to express what I need*—I allowed myself to believe easy lies. I deceived myself with ideas like *if I control everything and be a bully, our marriage will be bliss and I'll be happy because everything will be my way*. I had no instincts as to where to even start to address my misery, and I was way too scared to rock the boat. What if I messed something up and made it all worse?! I wasn't happy where I was, but I was comfortable. Isn't it strange to think that unhappiness can be comfortable? But it can be. Because comfortable isn't synonymous with good or fulfilling or desired or loved. It's what's familiar.

I wish I could tell you that the changes you decide to make will all work out on the first attempt, but I can't promise you that. I *can* promise you that whether you decide to keep things as they are or you decide to brave the change, it will be difficult. You get to choose which yellow-brick-difficult road you want to take. Staying stuck in the same place, clinging to the illusion of comfort, is hard. Exhausting, even. Waking up every day knowing you're settling for less than you deserve is hard work. And yes, stepping into the unknown, facing the possibility of failure, and confronting the discomfort of change is also hard. You get to decide which hard is worth enduring. So why not choose the hard that gives you a chance at a life that feels like your own? After all, why are you reading this book if not for some encouragement to rock the boat of your life?

Pre Reset Button Cameo and post Reset Button Cameo are two different people. Before the Reset Button, I was a lot of people: Cameo the Mom, Cameo the Athlete, Cameo the Wife. Now, on the other side of doing all of this work, I'm just Cameo. All of my roles coexist in a more organic, holistic way. All the battling between personas is gone. It's a less exhausting way to live for sure, but it's also more honest. It's a come-as-you-are mentality.

Through the permission and journey of the Reset Button, my decision-making process is now clear and refined and in complete alignment with my priority pyramid. As a result, my mistakes and setbacks are less devastating and often come with a faster recovery. The lessons I learn stick because of the thoughtful discretion in using the 3Rs. That all-too-familiar loop of destruction closes. Sometimes it doesn't even appear. I move forward in a way that's connected to my genuine self-interest, desire, and priorities. My confidence and resilience grow with each challenging situation I work through. The same can happen for you.

I've created a quick Hell Yes or Hard No Flowchart. I wish I could take credit for the language because I love it, but the "Hell Yeah or No" philosophy is one I learned from Derek Sivers's *Hell Yeah or No: What's Worth Doing*. The phrase sets the perfect tone because you don't want to make choices halfway. Use this chart to help you stay focused on asking the right questions. It's also important to run through the 3Rs at each question. Sometimes it isn't a clear answer without a little inquiry, authority, and a vision of what it looks like when it's done. Once you've rung out those 3Rs and had a few candid conversation trains with yourself, your choice becomes quite clear. It's Hell Yes at each stop or it's a No—a Hard No, for that matter. There is no in between.

DECISION-MAKING FLOWCHART
HELL YES OR HARD NO

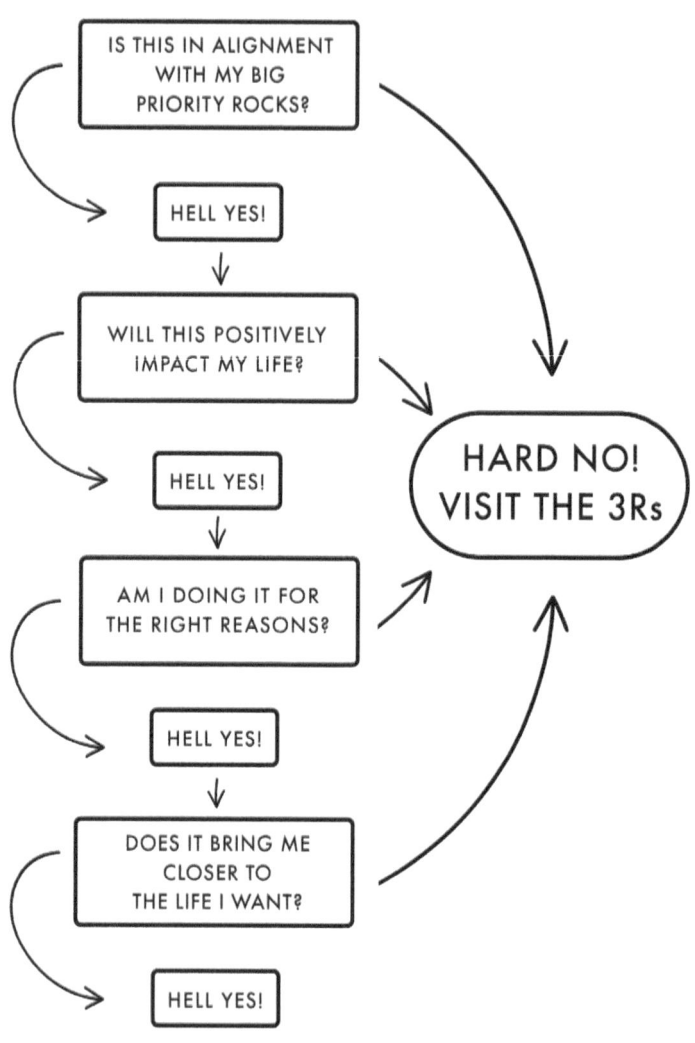

Maintenance

Use the chart when you begin this work. It can help to walk you through the process while you're still getting used to thinking this way. Eventually, you'll want to make it your own. Maybe you'll find you don't even need a visual aid. Maybe your questions will turn out to be different from mine. That's okay. Use this to get you thinking and see where that takes you.

MAINTENANCE

You Got This

I can't help but look back sometimes and wonder why it took so long to get to the point I'm at in my life. Then again, I'm mostly just grateful I made it here at all. Though it's impossible to know how my life would look without this process, I can make some calculated guesses based on the trajectory I was on before I began my Reset journey. Let's just say, it wouldn't be pretty. Most likely, it'd be an absolute shit show, and that's kind of a cute way of putting it. My drinking probably would've gotten worse. My resentment would've built. My relationships would have suffered, and I likely would have been even more unhappy, more lost, and less self-aware.

It's also impossible to know how my life would look had I made better choices earlier. Based on the immense change I've gone through over the last decade, however, I can imagine that everything in my life, from relationships to experiences, might be even richer now. Then again, some (not all) of those poor choices may have been exactly what I needed in those moments. They might have given me the motivation required to shift gears and admit that I was utterly lost.

It's easy to spend time ruminating on these what-ifs, isn't it? But the truth is, imagining either of those things isn't important.

The only thing that matters is what's happening right now. That's the only thing that's real. And each moment is an opportunity to begin again. I can't tell you how many times during the writing of this book I referred to my own process as a reminder of how to address a challenging situation, a difficult person, or the self-imposed pressures I put myself through regularly.

While we're on the topic of imagining, envisioning, and ruminating, let me make one surefire prediction: You will slip up. Let me say this again: You will sometimes revert to old habits. Resetting how you make decisions, especially when you've been using a framework that you've relied on probably since childhood, will be hard. Creating any new habit is hard. It's like any workout. It's uncomfortable at first. Unfamiliar. Remind yourself that, like any new workout, you've got to put in the reps to build the muscle. It's not magic; it's habit. And when you do "slip up," remember to be kind to yourself. There is no value in dwelling on it or self-pity. There *is* value, however, in seeing where you veered off your new path. Be honest with yourself. Did you fold when you faced a case of the "shoulds"? Were you worried about how you were being perceived? Was the change too uncomfortable to manage? Whatever you discover, go back and work through it. Then let it go and try again.

When I think back to November of 2013, the start of my life's implosion, I remember feeling like a monster. I was devastated and hopeless, dripping with shame. Greg was a shell of himself, drowning in pain. When shit went down with Greg one night in August of 2014, two weeks after moving to Florida, I felt scared and defeated. I was sure I'd ruined any possibility of living a fulfilling life and that I'd robbed our kids of their potential for leading a great life as well. At both of those crossroads, I searched desperately for any book, any blog, any story that had a theme or idea that I could identify with. One that ended happily. I searched for stories where a family like mine stayed together and rebuilt themselves into a healthy, stable unit. I found *one*, and I can't even remember the title or author. What I do recall is that it was written by a woman who had been betrayed by her husband. Despite the betrayal, she and her husband decided to choose themselves first, then to choose love and forgiveness, and, above all, to get to work from the ground up. She shared that after all of the pain, uncertainty, and decades of hard work—individually and with her husband—she was in a place where she could be at peace and grateful (notice I didn't say happy) that it all had happened the way it had. They were living a life they believed they wouldn't have been able to live without that catalyst for change. I couldn't imagine Greg or myself ever feeling that way about our situation, but I clung to that story. It gave me the glimmer of hope I needed to believe it was possible. And sometimes a glimmer is just enough to keep you going. If my book does nothing else, my hope is that my story, my discoveries, and this process has been that for you, the glimmer of light you needed to know that what you long for, the life you dream of living, is possible.

ACKNOWLEDGEMENTS

First and foremost, I want to thank Greg. You make me better in every single aspect of life, not by trying to change who I am, but by illuminating my strengths and validating my inner little kid. You are my king, my rock, my best friend, my hot rock star, my business partner, my annoying little brother, my bubble wrap, and my greatest motivator and supporter. Thanks for making me eggs and coffee every morning, for knowing the difference between when I'm mad or just hungry, and for being the greatest co-parent and co-pilot. I am forever grateful that you didn't give up when it was hard, ugly, and hopeless. You loved me when others might have deemed me unlovable. You exemplify what a true partner is. All this to say, I love you millions.

Thank you to Faith and Ben, who have given me the privilege of experiencing absolute unconditional love. You both have trusted me to lead, love, listen, and learn, understanding that I'm flawed and am figuring things out right along with you. Witnessing your incredible journeys is a priceless gift and I am beyond proud of you. I love you more than all of the sand at the beach.

To my mom, thank you for being my first phone call when I needed an ear, and for always having a hot cup of coffee ready. You've modeled what bravery and living boldly looks like. You embody the magic of "Bia" to everyone lucky enough to know you.

To my dad, thanks for instilling in me that "I can't never could do anything." You're still my biggest cheerleader, whether as the voice in my head or when I'm talking to you directly. You've always showed me how hard work and big energy create winners, and that quitters never win, and winners never quit – winning. Special thanks to Susan for putting up with you and making sure you stay healthy and somewhat "contained."

To Greg's family – you've loved and accepted me during all ages and stages of life. I have such gratitude for your willingness to help Greg and I whenever we needed you, whether it was when we were just starting out, when we needed help with the kids, or when we needed your support and understanding as we transitioned to Florida. Gary and Becky, thank you for your son. He is the man he is today because of the best parts of both of you.

Special thanks to "Bob" and his family. You were a loving example of stability when I needed it most. You helped me get (and stay) on my feet when it wasn't your job to do so.

To Jackie, our therapist, thank you for guiding us through the darkest chapter of our marriage with wisdom and compassion. Your support didn't end when the crisis did—thank you for going above and beyond when we hit bumps in the road and needed a gentle nudge to get back on track.

To friends and family, current and past, thanks for your kindness and forgiveness over the years—both when I deserved it and especially when I didn't.

Thank you to Julie for being patient and reliable, and for helping me find the courage to speak my truth and find the right words to do it.

To Jaime and Leah, thanks for your professional acumen and above and beyond effort.

Vanessa, your patience, guidance, and beautiful artistry brought this cover and interior to life.

Jesse, you have been a constant source of inspiration. You're my silent mentor, a leader, and a friend to everyone. Thank you for supporting my MISOGIs over the years, sometimes in small,

Acknowledgements

hands-off ways, and sometimes in life-changing ways - like your generous praise for this project.

Thank you, Judi, for being authentic, bold, fearless, and willing to share yourself with the world in that way. I've appreciated your guidance, our very important heart to heart, and your kindness in supporting this project.

Desi, you're a true badass and a consistent example of a powerful woman. Thanks for sharing your stories of struggle and triumph to help other women channel theirs.

JoAnn, you make moms feel seen, not just as caregivers, but as women. I've been so grateful for the opportunity to be a part of your community event. Thank you for supporting my book.

Lastly and maybe most importantly, thank you to you, the Reader. Thank you for spending your money and for taking your precious time to read my story. My greatest hope is that you find yourself in it.

YOUR RESET STARTS NOW!

Your journey doesn't end here. *The Reset Button* is just the beginning of a life lived with clarity, courage, and intention. To help you put these principles into action, I've created free downloadable worksheets designed to keep the momentum going.

Get your Free Worksheets at
www.cameoelysebraun.com/resources

Want ongoing inspiration and real talk about transformation, resilience, and reinvention?

Tune in to *The Cameo Show*, where I dive deeper into the stories, insights, and strategies that fuel meaningful change.

Listen to *The Cameo Show* on your favorite podcast platform.

ABOUT THE AUTHOR

In all things, Cameo Elyse Braun goes full throttle. Whether it's her passion for parenting, her deep love for her husband, her thirst for adventure, the seriousness she brings to her businesses, her commitment to music, or most recently, her deep desire to help people live their very best life, Cameo leaves nothing on the field.

It's that motivation and drive that propelled her to create The Reset Button, an innovative framework that guides people on how to live a life that's more aligned with where they are, who they want to be, and what goals they have. This is achieved through self-inquiry, permission, and self-interested decision-making.

The philosophy behind The Reset Button was born out of relentless self-work Cameo did after hitting her personal rock bottom. Motivated by a fresh start, she and her husband, Greg, moved with their two kids to Florida from Ohio. There, she voraciously studied and reflected on her life, seeking deeper fulfillment and greater personal growth. Among other formative decisions were her choices to give up alcohol and quit a very lucrative job. These two decisions opened up a world of possibility.

Powering her choices from a place of authenticity and vulnerability led Cameo to the bold choice of entrepreneurship—creating the Braun Mortgage Group with Greg. The Braun Mortgage Group is a dynamic and organically grown family business rooted in referrals and an impeccable reputation. Her professional success has also led her to pursue philanthropic work, allowing her to contribute to various charitable causes.

As a result of her successful business, her work on The Reset Button, and her related podcast, *The Cameo Show*, she has been invited to summits, workshops, Q&A's, and podcasts, to speak about entrepreneurship and The Reset Button framework.

Cameo thrives on pushing boundaries and fearlessly seizing fresh challenges. With an unyielding dedication to prioritizing her identity beyond her career, Cameo has achieved the highly coveted IFBB Professional Bodybuilding status, successfully faced the grueling 29029 Everesting challenge, and fulfilled her dream of recording a record at the iconic London Bridge Studio in Seattle, Washington.

Of all the hats she wears and roles she plays, however, Cameo's most important and proudest identity is wife and mom. Her family is her greatest joy and the driving force behind her pursuit of personal growth and success. The love and bond she shares with her two teens—who are compassionate, honest, strong, and confident individuals—serves as a testament to the power of intentional parenting.

Whatever is on the horizon for Cameo, she will continue her commitment to being a lifelong learner who works to empower others by sharing her captivating and honest journey. She is on a mission to prove that meaningful change in one's approach to life can lead to remarkable transformations and a fulfilling existence.

www.ingramcontent.com/pod-product-compliance
Lightning Source LLC
Chambersburg PA
CBHW030452100526
44580CB00006B/97/J